ENDING TERRORISM
Lessons for defeating al-Qaeda

AUDREY KURTH CRONIN

ADELPHI PAPER 394

The International Institute for Strategic Studies

Arundel House | 13–15 Arundel Street | Temple Place | London | WC2R 3DX | UK

ADELPHI PAPER 394

First published April 2008 by **Routledge**
4 Park Square, Milton Park, Abingdon, Oxon, OX14 4RN

for **The International Institute for Strategic Studies**
Arundel House, 13–15 Arundel Street, Temple Place, London, WC2R 3DX, UK
www.iiss.org

Simultaneously published in the USA and Canada by **Routledge**
270 Madison Ave., New York, NY 10016

Routledge is an imprint of Taylor & Francis, an Informa Business

DIRECTOR-GENERAL AND CHIEF EXECUTIVE John Chipman
EDITOR Tim Huxley
MANAGER FOR EDITORIAL SERVICES Ayse Abdullah
COPY EDITOR Matthew Foley
ASSISTANT EDITOR Katharine Fletcher
PRODUCTION John Buck
COVER IMAGE Getty

Printed and bound in Great Britain by Bell & Bain Ltd, Thornliebank, Glasgow

British Library Cataloguing in Publication Data
A catalogue record for this book is available from the British Library

Library of Congress Cataloging in Publication Data

ISBN 978-0-415-45062-1
ISSN 0567-932X

Contents

GLOSSARY

ANC	African National Congress
EIJ	Egyptian al-Jihad
EPL	Popular Liberation Army (Colombia)
ETA	Basque Fatherland and Freedom
FARC	Revolutionary Armed Forces of Colombia
FLN	National Liberation Front (Algeria)
FLQ	Front de libération du Québec
FPMR-D	Manuel Rodriquez Patriotic Front Dissidents (Chile)
GAI	Egyptian al-Gama'a al-Islamiyya
GIA	Armed Islamic Group (Algeria)
IRA	Irish Republican Army
LTTE	Liberation Tigers of Tamil Eelam (Sri Lanka)
M-19	April 19 Movement (Colombia)
MILF	Moro Islamic Liberation Front (Philippines)
MIPT	Memorial Institute for the Prevention of Terrorism
MK	Umkhonto (military wing of the ANC)
NPA	New People's Army (Philippines)
PKK	Kurdistan Workers' Party
PLO	Palestine Liberation Organisation
SA	Sturm-Abteilung
UDA	Ulster Defence Association
UVF	Ulster Volunteer Force
WMD	weapons of mass destruction

INTRODUCTION

Focusing on how terrorism ends is the best way to avoid being manipulated by it. Terrorism has been most effective as a strategy of leverage that draws its power from state action, and when democratic governments acquiesce to it, it is almost impossible to win. The ideal way to avoid this trap is to understand how terrorist campaigns have actually ended, and then drive towards that goal. There is vast historical experience with the decline and ending of terrorist campaigns over the past two centuries, yet few policymakers are familiar with it. Instead, officials tend to respond (very humanly) to popular passions and anxiety in the aftermath of attacks, resulting in policy made primarily on tactical grounds, undermining their long-term interests. Fear is exactly what terrorism is designed to exploit. When leaders make decisions primarily on the basis of fear they are perpetuating the natural dynamic of terrorism.[1]

All terrorist campaigns end. One way to nudge terrorist organisations towards their demise is to understand the closing phases of other organisations, carefully cull those experiences that apply to the current threat from those that do not, and act according to the lessons of relevant experience. While studying the history of terrorism is not sufficient to explain the threat the world now faces, it is necessary if we are to extricate ourselves from the counterproductive policies and narrow doctrinal disputes that are absorbing all of our energies.

Strategy is the art of distributing and applying military means to fulfil the ends of policy, yet thinking about the current struggle as a 'long war' connotes a virtually never-ending military battle between peers. If the efforts of these post-11 September 2001 years have taught us anything, it is that military means are insufficient to meet this threat. Instead, the United States and its allies need to employ the full, balanced range of national resources, the true 'policy in execution' that functions at a higher plane than strategy. Today, the concept of grand strategy, often mentioned but little understood, is even more relevant to counter-terrorism than it has been to many conventional military contests. More than 50 years ago, Basil H. Liddell Hart observed that the best way to formulate such a grand strategy is to look beyond the war to the nature of the peace.[2] Likewise, the best way to meet the current threat is to look beyond the international terrorist campaign inspired by al-Qaeda, beyond the military strategy the West has devised to answer it, towards a broader vision of how it will end.

A universal strategy for ending terrorism is by definition impossible. Previous attempts to devise one have tended to focus on singular means, such as brute force or capitulation, arising out of assumptions about the ideological causes that groups pursue. But the long-term threat to security posed by groups that use extreme violence, such as the al-Qaeda network, demands creative responses. While there is no substitute for 'local knowledge' and detailed expertise about specific organisations and cultures, failing to work across the seams of historical experience promotes parochialism and denies policymakers the cross-cutting concepts they need for countering terrorism.

We are learning to our peril that understanding war termination is at least as important as dissecting the causes of war. Likewise, processes of ending for terrorist groups hold within them the best insights into which strategies succeed and which fail, and why. Appreciating how terrorist campaigns actually end offers the chance to remove ourselves from the strategic myopia that currently grips much of Western counter-terrorism efforts.

There is much to be learned by studying the closing phases of other terrorist campaigns, and extracting common experiences and policy lessons from predecessors. Yet the wealth of historical experience with terrorism's termination is largely untapped. This Adelphi Paper posits five typical strategies of terrorism, and explains the particular challenges democracies face in responding to them.[3] It describes historical patterns in ending terrorism, to suggest how insights from that history might lay a foundation for more effective counter-strategies. Finally, it extracts policy prescriptions specifically relevant to ending the campaign of al-Qaeda and associated groups, moving towards a post-al-Qaeda world. In this case, as in countless antecedents, understanding how terrorism ends is the best route to a broader view of the campaign, and to thinking that goes beyond the shorter-term strategies of terrorism.

CHAPTER ONE

The Strategies of Terrorism

Terrorism's strategic logic is to draw enough power from the nation-state so as to enable a weaker, non-state actor to accomplish its political aim. Yet that is not to say that state governments necessarily determine the success or failure of terrorist campaigns. There are a number of direct and indirect ways for non-state actors to derive power from the state, and some of them do not directly engage with the government at all. In fact, study of the closing phases of terrorist groups – non-state entities that rely on violence against non-combatants – demonstrates that, in some circumstances, factors internal to these groups are most salient.[1] Policymakers often try to understand what 'works' against terrorism by studying the counter-terrorist campaigns of states, but this is only part of the equation. The history of terrorism reveals that the reasons for a group's demise may have little to do with the measures taken against it.

The strategies of terrorism are best approached by examining the intersection between objective, target and audience, taking care not to omit any of these factors. More specifically, the three dimensions of study comprise the overall political aims of a group, the nature of the direct state target of that group's attacks and the character of the audiences influenced by the violence. Distinguishing among these three elements is not as simple as it appears, however, as their relative weight varies and each may contain multiple layers and complexities. Their composition is determined by the political, social and historical context from which a terrorist group springs, and is as unique as the group itself. Thus, generalisations about the strategies of terrorism, like those for more conventional types of conflict, are inherently suspect and subject to exceptions. As in war, there is no substitute for detailed research into the nature and character of individual adversaries. Nonetheless, terrorism's 'triad' is equally vital to sound analysis.

Although non-state actors that use terrorism are smaller and less significant than states, their activities can be more difficult to parse. States share basic organisational principles, such as governments, national territory, populations and some element of control over the use of force. Groups that use terrorism are as different as the charismatic leaders that typically lead them.[2] They become *more* complex, not less, upon closer examination, like inert cells that come alive under a microscope. They are certainly *not* microcosms of states. Terrorism may be a tactic used by an inherently weak actor against a stronger one, but simple binary models are like pen-and-ink sketches of a dynamic process that actually develops in three dimensions. Nevertheless, certain themes emerge in analysing the purposes of terrorism. A convenient place to begin is with the familiar models of twentieth-century strategic studies. We will start with the scenario that unfolds when a group uses terrorism as a means of coercion or compellence to change the behaviour of a state.

Coercion and compellence

Always opportunistic, the strategies of terrorism continuously evolve, reflecting the nature of the modern state and the international milieu within which groups operate.[3] The phenomenon is subjective and hard to define because it is usually associated with trying to create public fear. Thus, terrorism is *intended* to be a matter of perception: as perceptions shift, so do the strategies of terrorism. Terrorism is like war in this sense: its nature reflects the social, political and historical context within which it occurs.

Strategies of coercion and compellence were well-suited to twentieth-century terrorism, an age of decolonisation, movements for national self-determination and the establishment of a bewildering array of new states.[4] In the aftermath of the Second World War, overstretched colonial powers, already under pressure for powerful economic, political and ideological reasons, found themselves vulnerable to terrorist campaigns. Brutal attacks exacted a degree of punishment that tipped the balance against the colonial powers and hastened their withdrawal, thus apparently succeeding in changing their policies. This was one reason why terrorism came to be seen in some quarters as an effective, even legitimate, tactic for national self-determination movements. Terrorism hastened withdrawals from the Palestinian Mandate, Ireland, Cyprus, Vietnam and Algeria, among other places; rightly or wrongly, it remains part of an enduring search for national self-determination in such hot spots as the Basque region of Spain, southern Thailand, Sri Lanka and Sudan. In the last century, terrorism was virtually always described as a challenge to the state.[5]

It is therefore hardly surprising that policymakers and scholars should think of terrorism primarily as a strategy of compellence, meaning the use of threats to influence another actor to stop an unwanted behaviour or to start doing something the group in question prefers. It is well-suited to nationalist movements whose aims can be expressed in terms of territory, particularly in situations where there is an occupying power. Seeing terrorism in this light is especially comfortable for Western policymakers, steeped as they are in the formal logic of game theory, air power and nuclear-deterrence strategy. It resembles a kind of counter-value targeting engaged in by non-state actors.[6] What could be more inherently coercive than a tactic that uses violence against non-combatants in pursuit of political objectives?

The parallels between terrorist violence and the state's use of force dramatically increased at the end of the century, with terrorism moving from its peripheral status towards more traditional (and more deadly) violence. Although the overall number of terrorist incidents declined in the 1990s, individual attacks became more lethal, with the average number of casualties per incident growing. Thanks to the global arms bazaar of the post-Cold War years, groups gained access to increasingly powerful conventional explosives, giving them much greater coercive power.[7] The toll from mass-casualty events such as the 1998 bombing of the US Embassy in Nairobi (224 killed, more than 5,000 injured) brought to mind the twentieth-century's theory of strategic bombing: the state's effort to use attacks on civilians to crush their will, shorten conflict and prevent the grinding attrition that Europeans had experienced in the First World War. Indeed, as its potency increased, terrorism gained a strategic impact in the West that seemed to meld with the logic of air-power strategy, targeting the morale of the civilian population in order to coerce states.

Thus, as important as it was, the shock of 11 September 2001 has had little effect on Western strategic thought. The basic axioms of strategic bombardment were easily applied to the study of so-called 'jihadist' terrorism, including the hopeless vulnerability of civilians to attack, the difficulty of effective defence, the benefits of sudden attack and the need for retaliation. According to this logic, terrorist attacks are seen as uniquely effective in forcing states to capitulate to the will of a group, particularly when the political goal is of greater importance to that group than it is to the state. The spectre of widespread terrorist use of chemical, biological or even nuclear weapons has further merged the study of terrorism – previously a peripheral nuisance chiefly tracked by regional specialists or dissected by philosophers – with strategic nuclear theory – the central theology of strategic studies during the Cold War. In keeping with the paradigms of their discipline, strategists have perceived in the increasingly deadly acts of terrorism a weaker power employing acts of punishment to manipulate a stronger power. Thus the intellectual framework of compellence continues to predominate.

Compellence seeks to change a state's policy. For example, it may endeavour to force states to withdraw from foreign commitments through a strategy of punishment and attrition, to make the commitments so painful that the government will abandon them. In classic game theory, terrorism is thus seen as a form of costly signalling that alters a state's perception of a group's ability to impose costs and its degree of commitment to a cause.[8] The ultimate goal of terrorist strategies is either to alter state behaviour or change the nature of the government itself. Political scientists argue that terrorists 'signal' through their attacks, as if they were weak adversarial states aiming to change a stronger state's policy or influence its population.[9]

At times terrorist attacks have appeared to succeed in changing state policy, as in the US and French withdrawals from Lebanon following the bombing of the US Marine barracks in Beirut in 1983, and the Israeli withdrawal from Lebanon in 2000.[10] Many also argue that the bombings in Madrid in 2004 led to a change of government in Spain and the hasty withdrawal of Spanish troops from Iraq. Likewise, some see terrorism in Iraq today as a foreign-inspired plan to force the United States out.[11] While each case is an oversimplification of what actually occurred, terrorism is meant to oversimplify complex situations: the interpretation is persuasive to many observers, not least those in the West, and that is a major reason why it is put forth by al-Qaeda spokesmen on the Internet and over the airwaves.

This intellectual construct has been furthered by recent Western analyses showing an increase in suicide tactics in terrorist campaigns. Long-standing suicide campaigns in Sri Lanka, Israel and Turkey were joined at the start of the new century by suicide operations in Russia, Chechnya, Kashmir, Indonesia, the United States, Iraq and Afghanistan. The strategic value of suicide attacks has been analysed by Robert Pape, for example.

Known mainly for his writings on air power, Pape argues that what he calls 'suicide terrorism' (in which he includes attacks on both military and non-combatant targets) has a unique strategic logic aimed at the political coercion of democratic states.[12] In the tradition of Thomas Schelling and Alexander George, Pape's thesis, expounded in *Dying To Win: The Strategic Logic of Suicide Terrorism*, is that suicide attacks aim to use the threat of punishment to compel target governments to change policy, particularly the withdrawal of their forces from occupied land. In his words, 'The heart of suicide terrorism's strategy is the same as the coercive logic used by states when they employ air power or economic sanctions to punish an adversary: to cause mounting civilian costs to overwhelm the target state's interest in the issue in dispute and so to cause it to concede the terrorists' political demands'.[13] Pape's book is widely admired, especially in US military circles, where suicide attacks in Iraq and Afghanistan are seen in exactly this light.

Given their twentieth-century experience with air power and nuclear-deterrence theory, Western policymakers and strategic thinkers find the logic of terrorism as punishment or attrition comfortably familiar. As a result, they tend to be oversensitive to strategies of compellence and blind to the other classic strategies of terrorism and their practical implications. Yet compellence emphasises only two parts of the dynamic of terrorism – the state and the objective – while saying very little about the role and nature of the audience. As a result, much about the strategies of terrorism is left out or ignored.

Understanding strategies of leverage

Provocation, polarisation and mobilisation are strategies of leverage that have been used repeatedly in the modern era, and for which terrorism is uniquely well suited.[14] Like compellence, these strategies have their roots in the political and historical context within which they arise.

The first, provocation, tries to force a state to react, to *do something* – not a specific policy but a vigorous action that undercuts its legitimacy. Provocation especially suited the nineteenth-century European political context, with its transition, in the aftermath of the French Revolution, from autocracy to popular suffrage. Urbanisation, rapid advances in technology and the availability of cheap print media all lent themselves to this approach. Terrorism, especially the killing of rulers and elites, was seen as a way of provoking a reaction by obsolescent autocratic regimes, thereby triggering a democratic revolution. Particularly in the second half of the century, following the failed revolutions of 1848, intellectuals turned increasingly to acts of violence to elicit a reaction that would spark change. The European philosopher of terror Karl Heinzen argued that 'the greatest benefactor of mankind will be he who makes it possible for a few men to wipe out thousands. The entire democratic party should make it its business to bring about this state of affairs.'[15] According to Serge Stepniak-Kravchinski, author of the autobiographical *Underground Russia*: 'In a struggle against an invisible, impalpable, omnipresent enemy, the strong is vanquished, not by the arms of his adversary, but by the continuous tension of his own strength, which exhausts him, at last, more than he would be exhausted by defeats'.[16] Joseph Conrad's classic novel *The Secret Agent* (1907) was likewise predicated on this thinking: in the words of the Professor, 'Madness and despair! Give me that for a lever, and I'll move the world!'[17]

Provocation was at the heart of the strategy of the Russian group Narodnaya Volya ('People's Will'). Many in the leadership of Narodnaya Volya believed that the peasant was overawed by the power of the Russian state. Their goal was to attack representatives of the tsarist regime so as to provoke a brutal state response, in turn inspiring a peasant uprising. Ironically, the group mounted its attacks at a time of unprecedented liberalisation, including the reorganisation of the Russian court system, the granting of limited self-government and, most important of all, the emancipation of the serfs. Beginning in autumn 1879, Narodnaya Volya launched six unsuccessful attempts on the life of Tsar Alexander II, failed operations that drew the group into the limelight and made its members targets for the Russian police and security services. A year later, every member of the leadership was either captured or on the run, with few hiding places and a greatly diminished capacity to plan operations. Despite police pressure, on 1 March 1881 a seventh assassination attempt in St Petersburg succeeded. In killing the Tsar Liberator, Narodnaya Volya did indeed provoke a legendary national crackdown, firmly reversing the trend of reform in Russia and setting the stage for the October Revolution of 1905. That is not to say that this act of individual terrorism led to the downfall of the Russian state, however: not only did Narodnaya Volya and its Socialist-Revolutionary successors fail to alter the regime in the intended direction, but they also found themselves marginalised and then targeted when the Bolshevik revolution eventually overthrew it. Narodnaya Volya's strategy of provocation was thus hardly a triumph.

Provocation is difficult to apply effectively, since terrorist groups often cause a state to behave in unpredictable ways. A government may be vulnerable to being manipulated or provoked into unwise or emotional action in the wake of a terrorist attack, as was the case follow-ing the assassination of Archduke Franz Ferdinand, heir to the throne of Austria–Hungary, in Sarajevo on 28 June 1914. The attack was not, in itself, exceptional. The tactic of killing political leaders had been endemic in the West for decades, including the assassinations of French President Sadi Carnot in 1894, Spanish Prime Minister Antonio Cánovas Del Castillo in 1897, Italian King Humbert in 1900 and US President William McKinley Jr in 1901. But because of conditions at the time, not least Austro-Hungarian fears about Serbian nationalism, the assassination had huge implications. Gavril Princip, the consumptive 19-year-old who carried out the assassi-nation, never meant to set off a global conflagration and was bewildered by what followed.[18] Terrorism on its own is limited in impact, but when it provokes a state it can indirectly kill millions.

Provocation is a classic, well-established strategy of terrorism, but it is frequently ignored by governments in the heat of the moment. Its purpose is to elicit an overreaction from the state, thus framing the forces of the status quo as aggressive and guilty, and the operatives as defensive and innocent. This is one reason why those who use terrorist tactics invari-ably describe them as defensive in nature, regardless of the situation or the nature of the cause they support. More recent cases of provocation include the Basque separatist group ETA's early strategy in Spain, the Sandinista National Liberation Front's strategy in Nicaragua and the National Liberation Front (FLN)'s strategy in Algeria.[19] Provocation always draws its strength from the reactions of the state.

A second strategy of leverage, polarisation, tries to divide a population and delegitimise a government. It is directed at the domestic politics of a state. The usual method is to attack members of the elite so as to incite a form of class warfare, but attacks can also take place across other political or ideological lines. Strikes against leaders or businesspeople, for example, often drive regimes sharply to the right, forcing populations to choose between the terrorist cause and brutal state repression. Polarisation strate-gies may also use terrorism to intimidate members of the opposite side into submission, or to gain strength relative to the opposition. The goal is to force divided populations further apart, fragmenting societies to the extent that it is impossible to maintain a stable, moderate middle.

Polarisation is a particularly attractive strategy against democracies, and appeared regularly during the twentieth century. Terrorist activities in Germany, Austria and Hungary after the First World War were meant to polarise and played a role in the coming of the Second World War.[20] Anarchist activities in Spain played a similar role in the coming of the

Spanish Civil War. Like provocation, polarisation often results in unintended consequences, when terrorist attacks act as catalysts for other types of violence, especially widespread civil war.

For obvious reasons, polarisation as a strategy of terrorism tends to work best in a domestic context. Polarisation was at the core of the violent Marxist/left-wing movements that prevailed in Europe and the United States in the 1970s, as well as the neo-fascist movements that followed them in the 1990s. Domestic left-wing terrorist groups that aimed to polarise communities include the German anarchist group the Second of June Movement, the Red Army Faction, the Red Brigades, the Weather Underground and the Symbionese Liberation Army. Right-wing groups include neo-Nazis in the United States and Europe, and some members of American militia movements such as the Christian Patriots and the Ku Klux Klan. In the 1996 Oklahoma City attacks, for example, bomber Timothy McVeigh appears to have believed that, by targeting the federal government, he could set off a race war within the United States.

A polarisation strategy may also justify attacks on other ethnic, racial or religious communities. Attacks by Sunni and Shia militias in Iraq spring to mind.[21] Likewise, the Armed Islamic Group (GIA) engaged in an extreme type of polarisation strategy during Algeria's civil war of the 1990s, killing as many as 100,000, including old people and newborns disembowelled or hacked to death.[22] Right-wing groups often have polarisation as their top priority: the British group Combat-18, along with its splinter White Wolves, urged members to kill non-whites (so-called 'aliens') to provoke a race war.[23] Other examples of groups that have deliberately acted to polarise societies include the Liberation Tigers of Tamil Eelam (LTTE) in Sri Lanka and the Provisional IRA in Northern Ireland. Like the strategy of provocation, attacks aimed at polarisation often have unintended consequences, leading a society to self-destruct.

In Latin America, polarisation strategies were used by left-wing groups such as the Argentinian People's Revolutionary Army and the Montoneros, but the classic case concerns the Uruguayan Tupamaros. In the early 1960s, Uruguay had a robust party system, an educated, urban population and an established democratic tradition. If democracy were an antidote to terrorism, Uruguay should have been immune. The Tupamaros, a small ultra-leftist urban guerrilla movement, adopted a strategy of targeting symbols of the 'imperialist regime', including businesses, airports and diplomatic facilities.[24] Gradually their attacks became more audacious, leading to paranoia in the business community and within the landed elite.[25] This drove politics to the right. The government temporarily

suspended all constitutional rights, and entrusted the defeat of the movement to the police. The police were unable to restore calm, and eventually,
in 1971, the government called on the army, which by the end of 1972, had
crushed the group.[26] Although terrorist attacks ended and the threat from
the Tupamaros was removed, the army then carried out a coup, dissolving
parliament and ruling the country for the next 12 years. In their short pre-
eminence, the Tupamaros executed one hostage and assassinated eight
counter-insurgency personnel in a campaign of kidnappings, robberies
and terrorist attacks. The right-wing authoritarian military regime that
came to power in 1973 killed thousands during its 12 years in power.[27] A
polarisation strategy drove the government to destroy itself.

The last strategy of leverage, mobilisation, is meant to recruit and rally
the masses to the cause.[28] Terrorist attacks may be intended to inspire
current and potential supporters of a group, again using the reaction
of the state as a means, not an end. Examples of mobilisation strategies
include the campaign of bombings and assassinations in the late nineteenth century by the anarchist movement, and the 1972 Munich Olympics
massacre, carried out by Palestinian nationalists. When terrorist attacks are
used to mobilise, they are not necessarily directed towards changing the
behaviour of a state at all. Indeed, unlike strategies of compellence, or even
provocation, a mobilisation strategy does not seek meaningful strategic
interaction directly with the state. Attacks aim instead to invigorate and
energise supporters of a group or cause and to raise its profile internationally, attracting resources, sympathisers and allies, so as to strengthen the
effort over the longer term.

The twenty-first century's globalised international community allows
movements to mobilise on a scale and at a speed never before witnessed
in history. Mobilisation strategies also get to the heart of why so many see
the struggle with religiously inspired militancy led by al-Qaeda as likely
to be multi-generational. Today's means of communications have gone
through a process of deregulation and democratisation similar to that
which occurred in France at the end of the eighteenth century. The result
has been a global explosion in chaotic connectivity comparable to the
sweeping changes that helped to deliver the popular mobilisation of the
French Revolution. People, ideas and violence are more easily connected
today than ever before.

Effective combinations of 'new' technologies, such as laptops and
DVDs, along with 'old' technologies, such as videotapes and mobile
phones, are facilitating political and social movements driven by newly
powerful ideologies. Not just access to information but the character of

knowledge and expertise is shifting. The Internet has, of course, led the way. It was designed during the height of the Cold War to be a redundant, decentralised, persistent and survivable network in the event of a nuclear attack. After the disintegration of the Soviet Union, the World Wide Web consortium was created to facilitate the spread of global connectivity. It has succeeded triumphantly. Throughout the 1990s, the use of the Internet at least doubled each year and, although the pace has recently slowed, global connectivity continues to grow, especially in developing countries.[29] For those without wiring, cell phones reach places where computers are hard to come by. They are especially popular in countries that lack a fixed infrastructure for landline telephones: in 2002, the number of mobile phones per capita internationally for the first time exceeded the number of traditional telephones.[30] The result of all this change in access to communications is creative anarchy, full of heady opportunity, but also pregnant with unpredictable change: a perfect context for mobilising followers, for both positive and negative ends.

The writings of social-movement theorists such as Sidney Tarrow, Charles Tilly and Douglas McAdam yield more insight into the form and purpose of a terrorist strategy of mobilisation than the traditional literature of strategic studies.[31] Groups that use terrorist tactics may evolve in the same way as social movements, using images of violence to alarm, inspire, impress, enrage or otherwise move individuals in a given population. In a global environment of democratised communications, increased public access, sharply reduced costs, increasingly frequent messages and the exploitation of images, groups like al-Qaeda are able to use a kind of 'cyber-mobilisation' to leverage the effects of terrorist attacks in an unprecedented way.[32] If a group is truly successful in mobilising large numbers of people, this strategy can prolong the fight and enable the threat to develop into other forms, including insurgency and conventional war. A mobilisation strategy is focused primarily on the audience; the target and even the political objective may change to suit the audience's needs. Hence, states in the West face ends and means of ideological mobilisation that differ from those that predominated during the era of revolutionary nationalism. While terrorist attacks are by no means a new phenomenon, their strategic logic and utility have changed to reflect the nature of the society in which they occur. Twenty-first-century communications are facilitating a return to individualised forms of violence, especially terrorism.

These four strategies – compellence, provocation, polarisation and mobilisation – are not mutually exclusive, and they may be joined by a fifth, de-legitimisation: the erosion of a state's fundamental legitimacy at home and abroad, so as to undermine it domestically or isolate it from allies. Only this last strategy has been consistent throughout the modern era, and it may be a crucial part of the other four. It points to the struggle for power and legitimacy that the tactic of terrorism always incorporates. A group may use a combination of several, even all of these strategies; but what a government does in response is at the core of their efficacy.

Democracies and strategies of leverage

Modern nation-states, even developed democracies, are not naturally designed to handle terrorism. Counter-terrorism strategies that are intended to prevent a state from being compelled by a group break down if the goal is to provoke a state, polarise a population or mobilise a constituency. And terrorist organisations may shift their approach to meet the demands of a fluid situation. Just as there is no evidence that terrorism is less likely to occur in democratic states (indeed, the data point the other way), there is likewise no evidence that democratic states are particularly adept at handling these multifaceted strategies, especially in the short term. Autocratic regimes, because of their rigidity, lack of concern for human rights and questionable legitimacy, tend to crush their challengers. Their mistakes and follies are well known. But the pressures on democratic states to respond to major attacks with repressive measures at home and overwhelming force abroad are arguably just as strong, albeit for different reasons.

Striking back with force immediately following a terrorist attack is reflexive, and it occurs for a plethora of motives. First, overt military retaliation is a kind of strategic catharsis. Sending air-strikes or military invasions seems fitting. It is extraordinarily difficult for any state not to answer force with force, and terrorist attacks by definition have a political motivation that challenges the current order.[33] Second, military retaliation responds to domestic pressure, the need to 'do something'. In the aftermath of terrorist incidents, public opinion virtually always supports military retaliation.[34] Elites respond to that pressure. Using military force sustains national morale and prestige, all the more so in retaliation for terrorism, a brazen and defiant act. There is much focus on the natural brakes on democratic war-making, but these are *accelerators* in counter-terrorism. 'Democratic peace theory' does not apply. Third, obliterating the perpetrators can be seen as meting out appropriate 'justice', especially when attacks originate from outside a state's territory (as is increasingly likely to be the case). With no reliable international enforcement of laws or norms, states must use their own military power to punish those who harm their citizens, and to deter others from doing the same.

A similar logic about the use of force against terrorism drives democratic states to react vigorously and sometimes unsystematically at home. Pundits who argue that controversial measures in the United States are unusual – the alert system, tighter access to visas, restrictions on civil liberties and so forth – are being hypocritical or absent-minded, or both. Europeans invented modern terrorism and then used it extensively. European leaders who have now happily passed beyond their period of anxiety during the nineteenth and twentieth centuries, when terrorist attacks by anarchists, social revolutionaries, fascists, leftists and nationalists/separatists threatened the stability of regimes, the continent and arguably the rest of the world, can hardly claim to be ignorant of the power and effectiveness of terrorism in challenging the state. New regimes in other regions have likewise tended to use overwhelming force in answering terrorist attacks, perhaps because the challenge is especially threatening in the early phases of a regime – and also because more restrained, phlegmatic counter-terrorism policies grow from experience, even trial and error. Notable examples of brutal crackdowns include actions by the post-colonial governments in Algeria, Sri Lanka, Egypt and India.

Democracies are often inept in their initial attempts at countering terrorists because elected leaders tend to make decisions that directly or indirectly reflect their constituencies. When people are afraid, a kind of generalised anxiety can propel policy and, as mentioned above, terrorism is specifically designed to heighten fear in a targeted population.[35] In the immediate aftermath of attacks, some democratic states have had more in common with authoritarian regimes than with mature democracies. But unless they grossly overreact and lose the support of their constituencies, democracies have a built-in mechanism that modulates their responses over the long term: the capacity to survive and learn. That is one of their crucial advantages in dealing with strategies of leverage. Even better, states can skip the trial-and-error phase and gain from someone else's experience – for example, by analysing common patterns of how terrorism ends and keeping their focus on that longer-term policy aim. This is what we will examine next.

CHAPTER TWO

Historical Patterns in Ending Terrorism

Looking at a wide range of case studies across different cultural and regional contexts, we can identify the point or points where a critical mass of factors led to the demise of a particular group. Doing so reveals the outline of a rough framework for thinking about the endings of terrorist groups throughout recent history. While there are no panaceas, there are more and less promising approaches. Pathways for decline have been influenced by factors both internal and external to a campaign: terrorist groups implode for reasons that sometimes are and sometimes are not related to the measures taken against them.[1] And the factors of importance in their waning are not always separate and distinct: sometimes more than one element is at play. But historical cases are nonetheless remarkably consistent, reflecting common processes in the downfall of these groups. Indeed, the recent history of terrorism reveals a relatively small range of endings – narrower, certainly, than the huge number of explanations for how and why terrorist campaigns begin.[2]

Myths about the end of terrorism

There is little agreement amongst experts as to how terrorist campaigns die. Indeed, a synoptic analysis of the debate would reveal that at least five myths permeate discussions about the end of terrorism. The first is that terrorism is endless, and that what is important and impressive about terrorist campaigns is not how they end but why they endure and demonstrate resilience. In the case of some long-lasting campaigns, this may

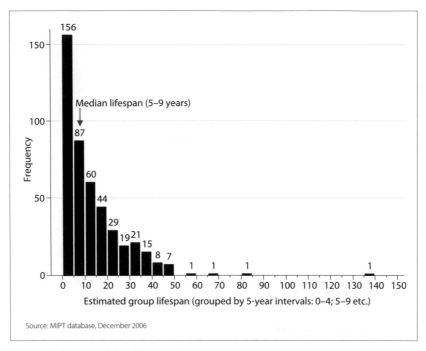

Figure 1: **Lifespans of durable terrorist groups**

well seem to be the case. But overall, are they really so durable? Studies of groups that use terrorism, across regions, cultures and historical eras, reveal that terrorism is by no means a promising vocation. Over and over, these case studies point to how difficult it is to maintain the momentum of a campaign. By any objective measure, the average lifespan of a group that relies on terrorist attacks is short. Examining the hundreds of groups listed by the publicly available Memorial Institute for the Prevention of Terrorism (MIPT) database, for example, yields the conclusion that the average lifespan of groups is between five and ten years, at the very most (see Figure 1).[3] Other estimates by well-respected scholars are even shorter.[4] There are few resources for studying groups that no longer fill the populace with fear. Governments tend to lose interest in a group when it is in decline, when the threat to the state has ended, leading to a dreary amnesia that drives states to make the same mistakes over and over again. The story of how terrorism ends is rarely written, but terrorist campaigns always end.

Second, many scholars, policymakers and commentators argue that terrorism is situation-dependent and can only be understood in the narrow and specific context of a particular group and cause. Arguments in support of this position reject comparisons both horizontally, across regions, and vertically, across time. Horizontally, the vast majority of work on terrorism has consisted of well-developed but narrow, descriptive case studies of specific groups, dissected by regional experts in such intimate detail that their broader relevance is indiscernible. The result is highly specialised books and articles tending towards the tactical. Others claim that groups defy historical comparison: some observers have labelled Islamist groups the 'new terrorism', for example, rejecting comparisons to predecessors whom they claim are fundamentally different.[5] Such claims seem akin to the notion that all snowflakes are unique and different, and yet the phenomenon of snow seems to have a variety of important properties.

Contemporary groups *themselves* consider cross-regional, historical comparisons compelling. Members of al-Qaeda, for example, have been far more interested in the history of their predecessors and how they met their demise than are many Western commentators.[6] Even as we have argued over 'new' and 'old', relevance and irrelevance, members of the al-Qaeda leadership have been discussing and writing about their predecessors, sharing the lessons of that history (as they interpret them) on the Internet, in pamphlets, articles and in books. There are scores of cross-regional, cross-cultural 'lessons learned' studies distributed by al-Qaeda and associates. Those translated into English *alone* cover groups as disparate as Baader–Meinhof and the Italian Red Brigades,[7] Harakat al-Dawla al-Islamiyya in Algeria (1982–87) and the Islamic Army of Aden Abyan in Yemen,[8] the Janjaweed movement in Southern Sudan and leftist movements in Central and South America.[9] Terrorist campaigns often display a kind of contagion effect, designed with the lessons of predecessors or contemporaries very much in mind. Naturally, there are differences and similarities between individual cases, but the value in studying them lies in determining what those differences and similarities exactly *are*. Group leaders consistently look beyond their own narrow and specific context. If we want to understand them and what they are trying to do, so should we.

The third myth is that terrorism's demise is simple and straightforward, because with enough force and oppression any campaign can be killed. This is decidedly not the case. Machismo and brute force seldom prevail on their own. There are frequently twists and turns along the way, at times including failed attempts to use direct force. As we will see below, some groups can indeed be crushed with violence, but if the approach does not fit the situation, no amount of force will change that fact. Terrorism draws in not only a group and a state but also an audience. Whether or not overwhelming force wipes out the group, the state is still left to deal with the audience, which may be an even bigger strategic problem.

The obverse of the third myth is the fourth: that dealing with the causes of terrorism will always lead to its end. Some analysts urge policies that will shift local public support away from al-Qaeda, for example, suggesting a long-term approach towards the movement's gradual decline. But in ending terrorism, the roots of a campaign are not as important as many people think. The weak relationship between beginnings and endings is the first thing that strikes you when comparatively examining cases where populations have become unwilling to support groups and their aims. The historical record flies in the face of the common belief that the causes of a terrorist campaign persist throughout its course, and are crucial to ending it. Far more often, the reasons why a group initially launches attacks against non-combatants evolve significantly over the course of a campaign, and are only loosely related to the reasons why it ends. Political objectives change as a campaign unfolds. Terrorist campaigns rarely achieve their initial goals, and external factors may be eclipsed by internal priorities.[10] Most commonly, the strategic 'outcome goals' that first spark a terrorist campaign, such as popular suffrage, self-determination, minority rights, a new system of government and so forth, are sidelined as a campaign unfolds by tactical 'process goals', such as revenge, retaliation, protecting sunk costs, consolidating a group and the need to show strength.[11]

The preponderance of research on the causes of terrorism, as compared to its end, is therefore misleading, even counterproductive. General ideological motivations and themes persist, but the commitment to pursuing them waxes and wanes. The launching of a campaign alters the strategic landscape, as well as the audiences that are observing it, in ways that are irreversible. When a campaign is already under way, it becomes imperative for policymakers to be aware of the give-and-take, to recognise their part in it, adapt to it and focus on a conclusion. In short, understanding the causes of terrorism is no more important to ending most campaigns than understanding the causes of wars is to ending them: naturally the question has some relevance, but it is overshadowed by the dynamic of the conflict itself as it unfolds.

Finally, the fifth myth is the belief that the best way to end terrorism is for states to engage in policies designed to win the sympathy of the populations from which terrorist groups emerge. This kind of 'hearts and minds' approach, adopted from counter-insurgency campaigns that accompanied twentieth-century occupations, can contribute to the end of terrorist attacks, particularly when a state successfully persuades a populace to stop underwriting the violence that is carried out in its name. Insurgencies in Malaya, Vietnam and Algeria are commonly cited in this context. But the role of the state in dividing terrorist groups (as opposed to insurgents) from their supporters is exaggerated.[12] While these methods are right and desirable for many other reasons, neither sending troops nor aid directly ends the violence. Comparative study of how groups that rely on terrorist attacks lose public support demonstrates that it is commonly *not* the state and its counter-terrorist policies that drive a wedge between groups and their constituents. Far more often, the crucial variable is the weaknesses or tactical errors of the group *itself*, which a state then highlights or exploits.[13]

Groups regularly self-destruct as a result of a range of mistakes and weaknesses, including operational errors, burn-out, internecine splintering, doctrinal infighting, targeting errors and revulsion or a backlash among their constituent populations. They are likewise obliterated by competitors. Governments can indirectly influence these processes: intelligent policymakers certainly cannot sit back and blithely wait for a movement to end in failure. Although groups may eventually collapse from centripetal forces, in the long run (to paraphrase Keynes) we are all dead. Groups can do a great deal of damage as they hobble along, especially in the twenty-first century when nuclear black markets appear to provide groups with alarming access to the means to acquire or construct mass-casualty weapons.[14] Instead, the argument here is that the best counter-terrorist policies have been those that are consciously synergistic with a group's natural tendency to implode. This may seem a subtle distinction but it has real-world policy implications: as will be further explained below, in ending terrorism, a government's top priority should not be to win people's hearts and minds, but rather to amplify the natural tendency of violent groups to *lose* them.

Other assumptions about how terrorism ends pervade our policies. Today, for example, national leaders focus on the capture or death of Osama bin Laden as a central objective in the campaign against al-Qaeda. Past experience with the decapitation of terrorist groups, however, is just beginning to be studied in a systematic way and, as we shall see, the relationship between decapitation and a group's demise is not straightforward. The use of force or other repressive measures has been successful in certain limited circumstances, yet the conditions under which it has succeeded or failed have not been examined for parallels with the current threat. Most observers assume that negotiations are irrelevant to al-Qaeda and associated groups, because it has non-negotiable, open-ended demands. Yet experience with other transnational campaigns with evolving or open-ended demands is hardly known. With respect to al-Qaeda and associated groups, Western counter-terrorist policies have been firmly grounded in hypotheses that do not withstand scrutiny from the perspective of how terrorist campaigns have actually ended throughout history.

People often try to understand what 'works' against terrorism by studying the counter-terrorist campaigns of states. But the reasons for a group's demise may have nothing to do with the measures taken against them. A far better approach is to study the closing phase of a group's campaign and answer the question: why did it end?

Examining how terrorist campaigns have ended

Although there are natural variations in the way specific groups end, demise generally follows six pathways, usually characterised by watershed events that lead to a diminution in the rate or lethality of attacks. These are not necessarily always distinct: sometimes a combination of processes – even an intersection between them – results in the decline or demise of a group. Historical cases are remarkably consistent in demonstrating a relationship between one of these six common pathways and the ending of a group, not least because each of the processes described engages with all three of terrorism's crucial elements: the state, the group and the audience. Some of the processes of decline are set in motion by the state, some by the group itself and some mainly by the audience. Terrorism is a tripartite phenomenon, even more so than war or other types of conflict, and thus the usual models of war termination do not apply. To reiterate, the goal here is to focus comparatively on the actual experience of groups in their declining months to study commonalities, so as to summarise and examine lessons that are relevant to contemporary policymakers.[15]

Catching or killing the leaders

First among the range of actions a government may take in pushing a group towards its end is to capture or kill its leader. Terrorist groups do sometimes meet their demise as a result of decapitation. The 'propagandist-in-chief' is more important for groups that use terrorism than it is for other types of violent political or criminal groups, even if he or she is not operationally directing the group's activities. The mouthpiece's primary purpose is to mobilise followers. If a group is well mobilised, then it is unlikely to rely heavily on terrorist attacks against non-combatants, which can be risky, controversial and counterproductive. Terrorist groups often feature an individual who exploits a sense of hope and a feeling of grievance or frustration, thereby streamlining the frustrating complexities of life and presenting terrorist attacks as a way of nudging history forwards to a new, more desirable future. Little wonder that governments like to target the top.

The effects of decapitation have varied, especially according to whether a group was hierarchically organised and oriented towards a charismatic leader. Cases of groups that were badly damaged by the capture of their leader include Shining Path in Peru, the Real IRA and Aum Shinrikyo. The Peruvian government captured Abimael Guzman, the charismatic leader of the Shining Path, on 12 September 1992, then displayed him before the media in a cage, wearing a striped uniform, recanting and asking his followers to lay down their arms. In the year following Guzman's capture, levels of violence in Peru fell by 50%, and, although the group has not completely gone away, it has generally declined thereafter.[16] The Real IRA's activities declined sharply after the British government arrested leader Michael (Mickey) McKevitt. From prison, McKevitt declared that further armed resistance was futile, and that the Real IRA was 'at an end'.[17] Shoko Asahara, leader of the cultish Japanese group Aum Shinrikyo, was arrested in 1995 and sentenced to death in a trial that ended in 2004. Aum Shinrikyo is best known for its use of sarin gas on the Tokyo subway in 1995, an attack that killed 12 people and injured some 6,000 others. Asahara's arrest was a devastating blow to the group, which was essentially organised as a cult of personality around the half-blind megalomaniac. Following the arrest, Aum Shinrikyo tried to rejuvenate, renaming itself 'Aleph' and recruiting new members, especially Russians, but factional disputes combined with heavier police scrutiny kept its activities to a minimum.[18]

There is considerable evidence to indicate that capturing leaders has been more effective than killing them in ending a group. The February 1987 arrest of four key leaders of Action Directe, Nathalie Menigon, Jean-Marc Rouillan, Joelle Aubron and Georges Cipriani, along with Max Frerot soon thereafter, effectively dismantled the group and put a halt to its activities. The capture of Otelo Saraiva de Carvalho and a large number of followers in the Portuguese group Popular Forces of April 25 (FP25) effectively ended their terrorist attacks. The Chilean group Manuel Rodriquez Patriotic Front Dissidents (FPMR-D) ceased to exist because of the arrest of its key leaders in the 1990s. Following a four-day siege, the 1985 arrest and imprisonment of eight leaders of the US group The Covenant, the Sword, and the Arm of the Lord put an end to it. That said, it is important how leaders are handled after they are apprehended. High-profile arrests sometimes backfire if jailed leaders are allowed to communicate with followers from prison, or when group members still on the outside attempt to free them. Examples include Sheikh Omar Abd al-Rahman (the so-called Blind Sheikh). Convicted for conspiracy in the bombing of the World Trade Center in 1993, he continued to communicate and radicalise followers from his cell. Comrades of leaders of the Red Army Faction repeatedly attempted to free them from a German jail.

Capturing a group's leader may be effective. The leader is often the source of inspiration for a group and thus its intellectual engine; their incarceration is an implicit answer to the illegitimacy of terrorism, and demonstrates the authority of the rule of law. But it is no guarantee that terrorism will end. Even successful, high-profile arrests targeting hierarchical groups can be overtaken by broader events. The Turkish government's capture of Abdullah Ocalan, head of the Kurdistan Workers' Party (PKK), in 1992, for example, was a huge achievement and seriously damaged the group, especially when Ocalan later advised his followers to refrain from violence.[19] Attacks declined significantly in the months immediately thereafter, and the group held to a ceasefire for five years. The invasion of Iraq in 2003 and the overthrow of Saddam Hussein provided an opportunity for the PKK to regroup in northern Iraq, however, and in June 2004 it began a renewed campaign of violence.[20] In addition to terrorist attacks such as car bombs in Turkish cities, PKK fighters were apparently given sanctuary by Iraqi Kurds and carried out conventional cross-border raids, including a September–October 2007 operation that killed 40 Turkish soldiers. A week-long Turkish ground incursion into northern Iraq followed in February 2008. The decline sparked by Ocalan's capture, a master-stroke of counter-terrorism, was dramatically reversed by broader destabilising events and conventional hostilities in the region.

Cases where a group has ended following the *killing* of the leader are less common. The two states most active in carrying out assassinations of terrorist leaders (apart from the United States in its campaign against al-Qaeda) are Israel and Russia. The Israeli government's campaign of targeted killings of Palestinian operatives in groups such as Hamas began openly in October 2000. Killings target not just the top leadership but also mid-level military and political leaders who are believed to be involved in planning operations. According to B'Tselem, an Israeli human-rights organisation, the Israelis have purposely targeted and killed about 202 Palestinians, and 121 people have unintentionally died in operations.[21] The question of whether or not the policy is justified is highly contentious. Many point to evidence of a drop-off in the frequency and lethality of terrorist attacks against Israeli civilians, although determining the degree to which this outcome reflects 'targeted killings' as opposed to other factors (such as the security fence) is impossible.[22] Others argue that targeted killings have attracted recruits to terrorist organisations, undercut Palestinian moderates and indirectly led to the election of a Hamas government in 2006. This debate is beyond the scope of this paper: whatever the benefits or drawbacks of targeted killings, they have not ended terrorism.

The other major campaign of killings of terrorist leaders concerns Russian targeting of Chechen leaders. Chechens killed in Russian assassinations have included Ibn Khattab, allegedly poisoned in 2002, and former Chechen President Zelimkhan Yandarbiyev, reportedly the Chechens' chief Middle East fundraiser, who was killed by a car bomb in Qatar.[23] In March 2005, Russian forces killed Aslan Maskhadov, formerly the democratically elected leader of Chechnya and arguably the only Chechen rebel leader with whom Russian President Vladimir Putin might conceivably have held talks. His successor, Abdul Khalim Saidullayev, was killed by Russian special forces in a raid on a Chechen village on 17 June 2006. Shamil Basayev, the notorious radical Islamist responsible for the 2002 Dubrovka theatre siege and the Beslan school attacks in 2004, was killed on 10 July 2006.[24] There are many other examples; indeed, only one of the movement's founding members, rebel President Doku Umarov, remains in Chechnya. The cost to the Chechen civilian population of the assassination campaign has been enormous. Human-rights abuses in Chechnya persist, and the cycle of retaliatory killings has spread the violence to the broader Caucasus, especially Dagestan, Ingushetia and North Ossetia.[25] Indeed, the Chechen situation is no longer distinct from broader violence and instability in the North Caucasus. Especially when considered beyond the borders of Chechnya, this campaign of assassination, like its Israeli counterpart, has not ended terrorism.[26]

Even in the short term, state targeting of a leader has sometimes backfired, especially in non-hierarchical groups where a ready successor is found or where the leader is killed in the operation and becomes a martyr. Determining whether or not a group will be ended by decapitation means thinking through the second- and third-order effects of removing the leader. Killing or capturing leaders often results in a struggle for succession. This reduces a group's short-term operational effectiveness, but it may also push it to adapt into a more effective, flatter, less hierarchically organised organisation that is harder to destroy. And as a new leader tries to demonstrate his credentials to other members of the group, levels of violence may actually increase.

Before targeting a leader, it is best to think through the question of who the successor is likely to be. In 1973, Israeli agents killed Mohamed Boudia, an Algerian who had orchestrated Palestinian terrorist operations in Western Europe. He was replaced by Carlos ('the jackal'), an even more ruthless and cunning man. It cannot be assumed that the leader waiting in the wings will be less effective or brutal than his predecessor. And the effect on the overall ability of a group to thrive is not foreordained. Will the killing of a leader result in martyrdom and the inspiring of more recruits? Measuring something that has not yet occurred is impossible, of course – assumptions about the so-called 'terror stock' are notoriously speculative. One fascinating and disturbing study of the killing of leaders of Palestinian terrorist organisations, for example, concludes that their deaths inspire more recruits than the deaths of Palestinian civilians killed in Israeli attacks.[27] Here, governments again have the advantage of being able to learn from trial and error: when a decapitation strategy results in a stronger movement overall, it is time to rethink the policy. The important strategic question for government policy is not just whether attacks are foiled, vengeance is exacted or a group is damaged, but also whether or not a policy of decapitation is helping to bring about the termination of a group in the longer term.

Crushing terrorism with force

The second way that states often try to end terrorism is through the use of brute force. This approach may involve aggressive military campaigns abroad (as with Israel's intervention in Lebanon in 1982) or domestic crack-downs at home (as with Turkey and the PKK), or some combination of the two (as in Colombia). Law enforcement is vital to any counter-terrorism strategy. Steady, law-abiding police work, particularly surveillance and prevention, can hold domestic campaigns in check and reassure the populace that legal norms persist; however, normal police work rarely *ends* campaigns, especially when they cross borders.[28] Most governments faced by major terrorist campaigns have been compelled to institute some type of emergency measures to answer the threat.[29] Repression is a natural response to terrorism for most states. As discussed in Chapter 1, it is as common a reaction on the part of democracies as it is for autocratic regimes, especially initially. In a sense, what could be a more natural and legitimate use of force than to avenge the very civilians whose suffrage is at the heart of state power? Whether held to be desirable or regrettable, there is nothing historically *unusual* in the exertion of overwhelming state force, which is after all nothing more than the modern nation-state responding to a threat in exactly the way it is designed to do. But does it work in ending terrorism? At times, domestic and international repression has indeed been effective in pushing groups towards their decline and demise. Historical cases include the Russian government's campaign against Narodnaya Volya, the Peruvian government's repression of Shining Path between 1980 and 1992 and the Turkish government's crushing of the PKK between 1984 and 1999. If the only goal is to end violence against non-combatants for a time within a given territory, then the use of force can be said to have achieved this repeatedly throughout history.

Repression seems particularly prominent in times of state transition: states that are insecure about their domestic or international standing seem especially inclined to use brute force. Post-colonial regimes, keen to establish their legitimacy, have used repression to put down challengers, as in Algeria, Sri Lanka, Egypt and India. Post-Soviet Russia under Putin used overwhelming force in the wake of a series of bombings of civilian apartment blocks in Moscow and Vologodonsk, blamed on Chechen terrorists.[30] Public outrage at the attacks, and support for Putin's strategy to end them, helped to cement his personal popularity. Putin framed the second conflict in Chechnya as a war against terrorism and used that motif in his promise to 'flush the Chechens down the toilet'.[31] By 2007, terrorism had indeed diminished within the boundaries of Chechnya, directly as a result of Russian military intervention, the assassination campaign and the elimination of all critical discussion of the conflict in the Russian media.

Yet the overall historical record of efforts to end terrorist campaigns through repression is chequered, for both democratic and non-democratic states. The use of force exacts a high cost. According to the Turkish government, during the crackdown on the PKK approximately 30,000 people died.[32] The Peruvian government had the worst record of human-rights abuses in the world in the late 1980s: over the course of the campaign against Shining Path, there were more than 7,300 cases of extrajudicial executions by government forces, over 45% of them in just two years (1983 and 1985).[33] The brutality of both the Shining Path and the government response set off a cycle of violence. The 2003 report by the Peruvian Truth and Reconciliation Commission claims that approximately 69,000 people died or 'disappeared' as a result of the Shining Path's campaign, half of them killed by the group, about a third at the hands of the military and the remainder either unaccounted for or killed by smaller militia forces.

Repression also regularly proves to be only a temporary solution, resulting in the export of the problem to another country or region, as in the spreading of violence from Chechnya to other parts of the Caucasus. It is especially difficult for democracies to engage successfully in repression over time, since such measures require distinguishing targets from the rest of the population, often undermine civil liberties and change the very nature of the state.[34] Keeping a domestic population anxious about the threat of further terrorist attacks and uninformed of the costs of repression appears to be crucial. But operatives may move to other territories, their ideas, once established, may persist, and the nature of the state engaging in repression may alter fundamentally. The use of repression against terrorism can undermine liberal or liberalising regimes, as with Uruguay's crackdown on the Tupamaros and its takeover by a military government in 1973. Massive state repression often kills many more people than the initial terrorist attacks.

There are multiple cautionary tales. In perhaps the best known, in 1965 the Egyptian government believed that it had destroyed the Muslim Brotherhood through a campaign of domestic repression. The organisation threw off numerous offspring, including Egyptian al-Gama'a al-Islamiyya (GAI) and al-Jihad (EIJ), two violent groups at the core of al-Qaeda whose leaders, especially Ayman Zawahiri, have been the intellectual force behind the al-Qaeda movement.[35] Egyptian repression clearly 'worked', to the extent that the terrorism of the Egyptian Muslim Brotherhood ended within Egypt, but the most extreme Islamist ideas within the group gained credibility and helped spawn the dangerous progeny that the world now confronts. When it comes to military repression, 'ending' terrorism in one territory or state may be a shallow accomplishment indeed. States have the power to obliterate entire populations, slaughtering thousands of civilians along with the actors responsible for terrorist attacks. In this sense, the overwhelming use of force by a state cannot *but* work, eventually. But short of that, whether or not repression ends terrorism depends upon how mobilised a population is for a cause, and how despised a regime makes itself in the course of its response.

Achieving the strategic objective
Although in the current climate it may be anathema to say so, the third way in which terrorism has ended has been as a result of success. A few terrorist groups have triumphed – that is, they have achieved their long-term strategic or 'outcome' goals and then either disbanded or adopted a more legitimate political form and stopped engaging in attacks against non-combatants. Given the nature of the tactic used, it is difficult to discuss this kind of ending dispassionately. And the fact that 'success' might be defined by the al-Qaeda movement's more grandiose aims of a united

Caliphate is truly antithetical to Western interests. But recognising that terrorism sometimes succeeds does not legitimise the tactic, and may even be a necessary prerequisite to reducing and eliminating it.

Instances of success are rare, especially when judged against a group's stated strategic aims. The effectiveness of terrorism as a tactic has been overstated in recent years, prejudiced by the dramatic spectacle of the 11 September attacks and the vigorous military response. Overawed by the threat, it seems, many analysts (especially in the United States) have drawn inappropriate parallels between group behaviour and state behaviour when assessing the strategies of terrorism, and have confused terrorism's short-term process and long-term outcome goals.[36] There is a crucial distinction between achievements that perpetuate violence and those that lead to its end.

For groups that use terrorism, tactical or process goals are innumerable and are associated with either gaining relative advantage from a position of weakness, or perpetuating the group itself. The former are most commonly studied, resulting in a strong perceptual bias and a degree of blindness about the evolution of campaigns. Because of the tendency to translate strategic theories developed on the basis of state behaviour directly to terrorist groups (as discussed in Chapter 1), observers assume that process goals relate to the bilateral conflict with a state. Yet terrorist groups are not the equivalent of weak little states and do not behave as if they were. They cannot assume even the most fundamental of state characteristics, namely survival. Some argue that terrorists engage in attacks as a costly means of signalling resolve to a state; while that is sometimes true, it is just as often the case that such signals are not aimed at governments, but rather at other observers in a wide range of other audiences.[37] Terrorist activities may not be aimed at affecting a state's behaviour at all, or the behaviour of actors related to or sympathetic to the state. Attacks are just as frequently directed at other, more proximate audiences, including competitors for a cause, current members of a group, potential recruits, active supporters, passive supporters or even neutral bystanders. Succeeding in the eyes of these beholders may enable the continuation of a campaign, and has nothing to do with ending terrorism.

Countless short-term objectives can be sought in the bounded reality of a terrorist campaign, all of which may be fruitful in perpetuating a conflict. Terrorist attacks can serve internal organisational goals, such as enhancing one individual's status at the expense of another, or external organisational goals, such as enhancing the position of one group at the expense of another. Suicide attacks against Israeli citizens have at times been used in a macabre competitive process between Palestinian factions.[38] Attacks may be launched simply to ensure the continued survival of a group, by showing ruthlessness or lionising a leader. The videotaped, ritualistic beheadings directed by the late Abu Musab al-Zarqawi and associates in Iraq come to mind. Likewise, the increase in attacks by the Abu Sayyaf Group in the southern Philippines following the killing of Abdulrajik Janjalani in 1998 was designed ensure the survival of the group following the devastating blow of Janjalani's death. Sometimes, groups simply want to exact revenge. McVeigh planned the Oklahoma City attacks for the second anniversary of the storming of the Branch Davidian compound in Waco, Texas, as a kind of vengeance against the federal government. Or terrorists may simply wish to shore up support: the LTTE, Sikh extremists, ETA and the Provisional IRA have all carried out attacks designed to attract the attention of far-flung diaspora sympathisers.[39] These are all process goals.[40]

Outcome goals, on the other hand, have typically related either to the nature of the state or the governance of its population. Groups may wish to bring down a specific government in order to replace it with a more 'just' form of governance. Maoist groups, such as Shining Path in Peru, the Naxalites in India and the New People's Army (NPA) in the Philippines, all seek a new society, where power resides with the peasants. The Russian social revolutionaries and their descendants, including the Italian Red Brigades and Action Directe in France, the Red Army Faction in Germany and the Weather Underground in the United States, sought to overthrow the capitalist system and replace it with a communist society. Fascist groups have sought to wipe out a race and ensure the dominance of the white majority. Some authors label Hitler's Sturm-Abteilung (SA, also known as the Brown Shirts) and Mussolini's Blackshirts terrorist organisations, but the later neo-Nazi groups in the US and Europe, including some members of American militia movements such as the Christian Patriots and the Ku Klux Klan, better fit this description.[41]

As we have seen, national self-determination was the most important goal of terrorism in the twentieth century. In other cases, groups such as the Tamil Tigers, the PKK and the Basque separatists have sought independence or autonomy within an established state. Groups also sometimes aim to bring about a new social organisation as a successor to the nation-state. The Russian anarchists fit this description, although their specific aims evolved and are not easy to summarise. Indeed, long-term aims may be difficult to visualise: the goal may be to bring on the apocalypse (as with Aum Shinrikyo) or to merely act as a catalyst to the forces of history (as with the Russian social revolutionaries).

Very few terror groups achieve their stated strategic aims. According to statistical research conducted for a broader book-length study, the overwhelming majority have failed, with only about 6% of groups that rely on terrorism showing full or substantial achievement of their aims.[42] In killing non-combatants, terrorism can attract people's attention, provoke tactical responses, lead a state to undermine itself and create a *cause célèbre*, but it almost never installs new rulers, inspires ideological change, takes over territory or constructs new institutions of governance (as terrorist leaders typically claim). Historically, by virtually any standard of measurement, terrorist successes, by which is meant campaigns that achieve long-term objectives and are then ended, are the rare exceptions.

There are, however, some well-known, even legendary, examples of groups that succeeded in achieving major political change and then either disbanded or moved on to more legitimate political behaviour. These are regularly cited, rightly or wrongly, by successors who hope to duplicate the outcome. The best known is Irgun Zvai Leumi, the Jewish organisation that fought to protect Jews in the Palestinian Mandate and to advance the cause of an independent Jewish state. Irgun attacks such as the 1946 bombing of the King David Hotel in Jerusalem hastened Britain's withdrawal from Palestine. Irgun was never a strong organisation, lacking both widespread popular support and resources; at no point did it pose a serious military threat to the British. But at the heart of its power was a sophisticated propaganda war, what one prominent member labelled its 'campaign of enlightenment', directed especially towards a sympathetic international audience in the wake of horrifying evidence of the plight of the Jewish people during the Second World War. The British were economically crippled in the early post-war years and withdrawing from other commitments elsewhere. The decision to quit Palestine was ripe for implementation and, within the highly politicised international context, Irgun's attacks were an effective catalyst. The group disbanded with the creation of the state of Israel in 1948.

The African National Congress (ANC) is another example of a successful group that used terror tactics. The ANC created a military wing, Umkhonto (MK), and, after nearly five decades of non-violent resistance, turned to terrorist attacks in 1961. It fought to end apartheid and establish a multiracial state in South Africa. The MK's last attack occurred in 1989, and the ANC became a legitimate political party in 1990, with its leader, Nelson Mandela, elected first president of post-apartheid South Africa. But the question of cause and effect in these two examples (as in others) is complex: there is a great deal of evidence to indicate that both strategic outcomes were achieved at least as much *despite* the use of terrorism as because of it. In the ANC case, for example, the extensive pressures that led to the end of apartheid, including economic, cultural and sporting sanctions by the international community, a revolt among white English- and Afrikaner-speaking youth, a political revolt among members of the South African National Party and widespread, grassroots frustration and organisation on the part of the black community all undermined the legiti- macy of the policy of apartheid and were more important than terrorist attacks in ending it.[43]

These and other oft-cited cases lead to the conclusion that the keys to strategic success for terrorist groups are fourfold.[44] Firstly (and most obviously), groups must have well-defined and realisable aims; i.e., it is impossible to succeed if no one knows what your aims are. This is one reason why the most successful groups in the twentieth century were those whose objectives related to territory and the governance of the nation-state, both of which are tangible concepts, widely understood and at the heart of the modern international system. Secondly, groups are best able to succeed when they can convince major powers of the legitimacy of their cause and gain their backing, morally or materially or both. As is the case with insur- gencies, terrorist campaigns benefit tremendously from outside support.[45] Thirdly, groups that use terrorism can only succeed when their actions comport with broader historical, economic and political changes that are occurring anyway in the international system. It is no coincidence that the most successful cases in the twentieth century are those where a colo- nial power found itself unable to hold onto its territories – as in Vietnam, Cyprus, Algeria and Ireland. To determine whether or not a cause is likely to succeed over the long term, therefore, the best 'intelligence' is an objec- tive awareness of the changing international political context. Finally, terrorism succeeds best when it is part of a broader campaign and the tactic is replaced by more legitimate means, especially popular uprisings, guerrilla warfare and insurgency. A weak and illegitimate tactic, terrorism *alone* has never succeeded in achieving strategic ends.

Moving towards a legitimate political process
The fourth means by which terrorism can be said to have ended revolves around the concept of a negotiated settlement. Groups that entered into negotiations with the state have included the Provisional IRA (the 1998 Good Friday accords), the Palestine Liberation Organisation (PLO) (progress in the peace process during the 1990s) and the LTTE (which engaged in talks with the Sri Lankan government between 2002 and 2007).

As these cases indicate, however, a process of negotiation is by no means a panacea, with many setbacks along the way. In determining when and how negotiations end terrorism, idealistic platitudes are as misguided as righteous condemnations of the evils of terrorism. Clichés about talking to terrorists do not hold up: after groups survive past the five- or six-year mark, it is not at all clear that refusing to negotiate with them shortens their violent campaigns any more than entering into negotiations prolongs them. Negotiations can facilitate a process of decline, but they have rarely been the single factor driving an outcome.

Looking at the recent history of terrorist campaigns, there are a number of interesting patterns with respect to negotiations. Firstly, there is a direct correlation between the age of the group and the probability of talks.[46] The longer a group exists, the greater the likelihood that a peace process will begin, as groups become desperate for a resolution and governments come to realise that these non-state actors cannot be avoided or crushed. But this does not mean that most groups that engage in terrorist attacks negotiate: only about one in five groups of *any* age have entered into talks on strategic issues.[47] Talks with groups that use terrorism are the exception, not the rule. Secondly, the vast majority of negotiations that do occur yield neither a clear resolution nor a cessation of the conflict. A common scenario has been for negotiations to drag on, occupying an uncertain middle ground between a stable ceasefire and high levels of violence. About half of the groups that have negotiated in recent years have continued violent actions as the talks have unfolded, usually at a lower level of intensity and frequency. Negotiations seem to be more effective in gradually driving a group towards decline than single-handedly occasioning its abrupt end.

Negotiations with terrorist groups have occurred most easily in situations where the group perceives itself to be losing ground. This may transpire for a number of reasons: it may reflect competition with other groups (as with the PLO, with the rise of competitors in the intifada); infiltration by government agents (as with the Provisional IRA); an undercutting of support (as with the LTTE immediately after the 11 September attacks); or a backlash by the group's own constituency (most often due to targeting errors). Indeed, increasing civilian casualties directly caused by a group within its constituency are a common impetus for talks.

A wide range of variables can determine the efficacy of negotiations, including the nature of the organisation (hierarchical groups have an advantage over groups that cannot control their members' actions), the nature of the leadership (groups with a strong leader have an advantage over those that are decentralised), and the nature of public support for the cause (groups with constituencies who have tired of violence are more likely to compromise). There must also be negotiable aims, which is more likely with territorially based groups than with those that primarily espouse left-wing, right-wing or religious/spiritual ideologies – although experience indicates that, whatever their claims, groups' goals typically evolve. The most important condition is that both sides sense that they have achieved a situation where additional violence is counterproductive. William Zartman's concept of a 'hurting stalemate' in civil wars seems to apply here; from the perspective of a challenger group that mainly uses terrorism, however, this stalemate reflects a political rather than a military status. Generally, groups are more likely to compromise if their popular support is waning. Since terrorism is a means of political mobilisation, it is crucial to determine the degree of popular support for a group when deciding whether negotiations are likely to yield results. Likewise, if a group perceives that the domestic constituency of a state is shifting in ways that serve its interests, it will wait before entering into negotiations. The degree of mobilisation for a cause, especially the ways in which popular support and interest are changing, is a crucial variable in determining whether or not negotiations will be promising.

Negotiations instantly change the 'narrative' of the terrorist group's violence, affecting its ability to attract or maintain supporters. The direction in which this change proceeds may not be obvious; the relationship between talks and terrorism is not straightforward. States may wish to avoid the appearance of legitimising a non-state group, thereby enraging their own citizens. But avoiding talks may in turn enhance a group's position with its constituents, strengthening the argument that the only way to get the attention of the state is to commit increasingly violent acts. States should assess the likely effects on a group's cohesion and viability. By refusing to talk about the issue that is of concern to a group (if there is one) a government yields the agenda to that group just as surely as if it entered into discussion of the issue, since either position represents the manipulation of state behaviour through the killing of its civilians.[48] While it is important to concentrate on ending attacks in the short term, the story that is being put forth by a group in order to justify its violence may be more central than any physical actions to its long-term viability, and may be more vulnerable to counter-attack.

Groups often splinter as a result of talks, and this can be either a good or a bad thing depending on the circumstances. Examples of this pattern include the Provisional IRA and the PLO. Dividing terrorist groups into factions has either isolated the most radical elements, which has the advantage of making them easier to target, or increased the violence against civilians in the short term, as radical factions try to demonstrate their viability by carrying out new attacks. But because negotiations in the wake of terrorist acts are always controversial, splintering has sometimes occurred on the status quo side instead: this was the case, for example, in South Africa (with the Afrikaner white-power group Farmers' Force, or Boeremag) and in Northern Ireland (with the Ulster Volunteer Force (UVF)). Weak governments are often threatened by conciliatory approaches by terrorist groups. The most extreme case of splintering on the status quo side is in Colombia, where the signing of peace accords in 1984 between the government and the Popular Liberation Army (EPL) resulted in the formation of right-wing paramilitary groups that opposed the granting of political status to the EPL. Before long, leftist groups, paramilitary groups and the Colombian Army had all stepped up their attacks, unravelling the peace, increasing violence and further dividing political actors. In negotiations the long-term goal (a viable political outcome) is often at odds with the short-term goal (a reduction in violence).

Indeed, there is no guarantee that the military situation will be improved by negotiations, especially in the short term. Groups sometimes enter into talks disingenuously, to ease the pressure of counter-terrorist measures and to rearm. Some IRA groups or members (probably of the Provisional IRA) continued to procure weapons following the 1998 Good Friday agreement, buying guns in the United States and attempting to import AN-94 rifles from Russia.[49] The Basque group ETA announced a ceasefire in 1998, following a public backlash against the killing of a popular young councillor, and then renounced it in 1999, claiming that it had wanted a reprieve from government pressure in order to rearm. The LTTE, having repeatedly entered into peace talks and ceasefires with the Sri Lankan government, has regularly built up its military capabilities during these periods. Negotiations are best seen as a way of shifting the relationship between a government and a group into a different paradigm, managing the relationship while a group loses momentum or makes mistakes that can be exploited.

Other factors have also been important to the success or failure of negotiations. These include the presence or absence of suicide campaigns: the use of suicide attacks makes resolution especially problematical, as it reduces the willingness or ability of factions to live alongside each other. The presence of strong leaders on both sides of the talks increases the likelihood of success. Although it may be desirable for other reasons, forcing a leadership change often complicates talks, since it may result in a more diffuse organisation that is more difficult to parley with. Finally, the presence or absence of third-party states is important, as are mediators, outside guarantors and other external actors willing to push along or support the negotiations. The 1985 Anglo-Irish Agreement and subsequent efforts by the Irish government to influence and support Northern Irish Republicans were crucial to the signing of the Good Friday accords.

Spoilers receive a great deal of attention in the context of negotiations, as terrorist attacks by splinter groups or disgruntled factions aim to derail or destroy talks. Clearly, talks that are not marred by spoiler attacks promise better outcomes. One study examining 14 peace agreements signed between parties to civil wars from 1988 to 1998 concluded that, if terrorist attacks occurred in association with the talks, only one in four treaties were put into effect. If they did not occur, 60% took effect.[50] Campaigns that rely primarily on terrorist attacks may be even harder than civil wars to resolve. But the cause and effect of spoiler attacks is hard to determine. Spoiler violence is often directed at gaining power within a movement at a time of change or opportunity, rather than seeking to undermine the talks themselves.

Even when they are clearly directed at disrupting talks, spoilers may not have the desired effect. If a foundation of popular support for talks exists, there are strong outside guarantors and the negotiators are identified with the process itself, terrorist 'spoiler' attacks can actually strengthen the commitment to negotiations, rather than undermine it. The Northern Ireland peace process comes to mind. Terrorist incidents were frequently timed to coincide with developments in the talks, but effective public-relations efforts by all parties meant that public anger was directed against the spoilers, making the negotiations more resilient, not less. When spoiler violence occurs, therefore, whether or not interested parties inside and outside the talks label it illegitimate appears to make a difference, especially when the response is outrage at the attackers themselves and renewed support for the talks.

Negotiations have many benefits, and are a common element in the gradual ending of terrorist groups. Given the small number of operatives needed to continue terrorist attacks, however, violence almost never ends instantaneously. Judging the efficacy of negotiations is thus not simply a matter of whether or not they result in the end of violence in the short term. The most likely result for a government that chooses to negotiate and can withstand domestic pressure is long-term management of the threat over a lengthy period of gradual decline. Unlike civil wars and inter-state conflicts, where fighting normally stops while talks proceed, negotiations during terrorist campaigns redirect the contest into a less violent channel as the campaign winds down for other reasons. Talks carry risks and can pose a serious challenge for a democratic state that enters into them without a firm domestic mandate to do so, managed expectations and a back-up plan for when terrorism recurs. From the state's perspective, while negotiations are not a promising tactical means to end terrorist campaigns by themselves, if well handled they are nonetheless a wise and durable strategic tool for managing violence, splintering the opposition and facilitating its longer-term decline.

Implosion and loss of popular support

The fifth way terrorist groups die is because they become cut off from their source of sustenance, or implode. Firstly, and arguably most importantly, groups regularly fail to move beyond the first generation, for reasons that are both internal and external to them.

Many argue that terrorist activity has lifecycles. Individual groups go through phases of emergence, escalation and de-escalation directly connected to their ability to attract new blood. But the global links, moral or physical, between groups are also vital. David Rapoport observes that, over the course of modern history, waves of international terrorist activity have lasted about a generation, or approximately 40 years. In the modern era, Rapoport sees four 'waves': the anarchist wave initiated in the 1890s, the anti-colonial wave following the Second World War, the New Left wave begun in the 1970s and what he terms the 'religious wave' under way today. Central to these generational waves are their global nature and the common predominant energy (or ideology) that shapes participating groups' characteristics and mutual relationships. Factors critical to perpetuating Rapoport's global waves are a transformation in communications or transportation patterns and a charismatic doctrine or culture.[51] Ideological connections are not sufficient in themselves: groups that are linked to the same radical ideas also emerge out of a sense of opportunity gained from observing the tactical successes of other groups.[52] But, again, the point of transition from one generation to another is crucial, as the first generation of leaders age and tire, their revolutionary message lacks clarity or loses appeal and another generation fails to take their place.

The generational phases of terrorist campaigns are thus related to demographic patterns and the growth of radical ideologies internationally.[53] Some grievances have been easier to translate from one generation to another; in the twentieth century, those connected either to territory or to the identity of a group's supporters or constituents conveyed well.

Left-wing ideologies have had less staying power than ethno-nationalist causes. The left-wing groups of 1970s Europe were notorious for their inability to articulate a clear vision of their goals, which could be handed down to successors after the first generation of leaders had been captured or eliminated. As the leftist/anarchist philosophies of groups such as the Red Brigades, the Second of June Movement, the Japanese Red Army and the Weather Underground became bankrupt or unintelligible, they found it increasingly difficult to attract new recruits, especially after the dissolution of the Soviet Union.[54]

Right-wing groups have also had difficulty lasting over generations. This is probably a reflection of their peripatetic nature and their decentralised cell structures – though it should also be borne in mind that these characteristics themselves mean that tracking groups' evolution from generation to generation presents prodigious challenges, which may have the effect of limiting our knowledge of their lifespans. Examples of such groups include the numerous neo-Nazi groups in the United States, such as the Christian Patriots, the Aryan Nations, the Ku Klux Klan, The Order (a short-lived faction of Aryan Nations) and the Hammerskin Nation; the Anti-Zionist Movement, Combat 18, the Germany People's Union and the National Front in Europe; and the National Warriors of South Africa. Since the racist philosophies of many of these groups can persist long after the disappearance of the group itself, however, the re-emergence of the same cause violently pursued under a different name or organisational structure is common. European neo-Nazi groups and right-wing Christian militia groups in the United States declined sharply at the end of the century, though there is reason to fear a resurgence in the future.[55]

A second cause of self-destruction is infighting and factionalisation. The pressures of continuing a campaign have regularly led to counterproductive and dysfunctional behaviour among a group's members, including struggles over doctrine, operations, leadership and tactics. Individuals may struggle for predominance within a group (as with the GIA in Algeria in 1994–95) or over the nature or pace of operations (as with the Provisional IRA or the Red Army Faction).[56] When groups break up into factions, internecine competition may make them more concerned with stamping out competitors than furthering a common cause. Clashes between Palestinian groups in the second intifada come to mind here.

Another common source of internal dispute stems from the nature of the group's ideology or doctrine. Because of their impermanence and relative weakness, and the blatant illegitimacy of their attacks on non-combatants, terrorist groups are almost uniquely dependent on the 'story' that justifies their actions and existence. Members who argue over the nature of that crucial narrative often turn against one another. Ideological disputes have been an important factor in the demise of groups as disparate as the Japanese Red Army, the Second of June Movement, Combat-18 and the Front de libération du Québec (FLQ).

Sometimes, the story becomes unconvincing even to members, who burn out or come to the conclusion that their aims are not being advanced by terrorist tactics. Some may accept an exit offered by the state. In Italy, 'repentance' laws passed in 1980 and 1986 famously contributed to the ending of the Red Brigades and numerous smaller rivals. In Colombia, the April 19 Movement (M-19), under pressure from the government and paramilitary groups, agreed to an amnesty before transforming itself into a political party, Democratic Alliance M-19, to pursue a reform agenda and advocate on behalf of the poor.[57] Most groups are unable to overcome these centrifugal forces, and this is an important reason why the vast majority of groups that rely on terrorist attacks soon self-destruct.

A third reason for self-destruction is the tendency of terrorist groups to lose control over operations. This is a classic problem, especially when groups are faced with police or military pressure that makes it difficult to maintain both personal security and operational efficiency. Groups seeking to evade detection often adopt more horizontal structures so as to limit the damage to a hierarchy if a member is caught. Dating at least to the late nineteenth century, networked terrorist organisations are not new. They can compartmentalise information and keep themselves from detection by the state, and may even be better able to carry out attacks, especially small operations launched against soft targets. However, the sum of these tactical networked operations may not necessarily add up to a logical strategy that advances the purposes of the broader organisation. An inability to control rogue killings doomed the Protestant paramilitary groups the UVF and the Ulster Defence Association (UDA), for example. Uncoordinated, poorly planned or badly targeted operations increase the likelihood of a popular backlash against a group.

Without some level of popular support, a group quickly dies. Popular support has dissipated in recent history for a number of reasons, including intimidation (as in Chechnya), the offer of a better alternative (reform movements, employment programmes and amnesties, as in Italy) or the bankruptcy of the group's ideology (as with many of the Marxist groups supported by the Soviet Union and its Eastern European allies). A key source of marginalisation, however, is the organisation's own errors, especially miscalculations in targeting. Terrorist attacks, although shocking and tragic, are designed to mobilise support among a target constituency by demonstrating strength, exploiting hatred of the target or providing an avenue for public retribution. Sometimes, however, the intended effect is not achieved. Misguided, poorly timed, overly brutal or mistakenly targeted attacks can lead to revulsion among a group's actual or potential political constituency and lead to its decline and demise.

Examples abound. The Omagh bombing by the Real IRA in 1998, which killed 29 people including nine children, led to outrage and saw the local community withdraw its support. The Beslan school seizure badly eroded support for the Chechen cause in Europe, making it easier for the Russian government to act with impunity in Chechnya. Revulsion at the killings of tens of thousands of civilians between 1981 and 1995 undermined popular support for the Sikh separatist movement in India. Another famous case was the kidnap and subsequent killing in 1978 of former Italian Prime Minister Aldo Moro by the Red Brigades. Following the killing, the Italian government began a vigorous counter-terrorism campaign, popular support for the Red Brigades dried up and the group began to crumble. The killing of Moro, a popular politician whose numerous letters from captivity were widely publicised, was a colossal strategic error that doomed the group. The Red Brigades declared its own end in 1984, when four of its leaders wrote a communiqué from jail claiming that 'the international conditions that made this struggle possible no longer exist'.[58] Another notorious example of a misguided operation was the killing of 62 people (most of them tourists) in the town of Luxor in southern Egypt in November 1997. The Islamist group al-Gama'a al-Islamiyaa (GAI) had intended to strike a blow against Egypt's tourist economy, provoking the Egyptian government into a crushing response that would draw more people into sympathy with the group. Instead, the brutal attack, whose victims included young children, honeymooners and a man beheaded in front of his daughter, outraged the Egyptian public. According to Lawrence Wright, in the five years before Luxor Islamist terrorist groups killed more than 1,200 people, many of them foreigners; after Luxor, attacks by Islamists in Egypt abruptly stopped.[59]

Moving to other malignant forms

The sixth and final way terrorism can 'end' is when the violence continues, but assumes another form. Groups that use terrorism at times reorient their behaviour, moving away from politically motivated attacks on civilians or non-combatants towards criminality (as with Abu Sayyaf or the Revolutionary Armed Forces of Colombia (FARC)) or towards full insurgency and even conventional war (as with the Algerian FLN or the Kashmiri groups Lashkar-e-Tayiba and Jaish-e-Mohammed).

Distinguishing between terrorism and criminal behaviour is not simply a case of determining whether a group is driven by profit or politics. Groups are increasingly engaging in so-called precursor crimes, criminal activities such as fraud, petty crime, identity theft, counterfeiting, drug-trafficking and arms trading, which offer quick riches and the potential to finance operations independently of traditional sources such as states and diasporas.[60] Study of civil wars indicates that they last longer when combatants have access to resources generated through contraband goods such as opium, diamonds or coca; it seems likely that the same applies to terrorist groups and their campaigns.[61] Particularly in the wake of the end of the Cold War, with its reduction in state sponsorship for terrorist groups, the pressure on groups to diversify their sources of income, both legal and illegal, has increased. Alternatively, groups or individuals that gravitate towards criminal behaviour may be falling back on established competencies at a time when others are demobilising or ending violence. This was the case with paramilitaries in South Africa and Northern Ireland, for example.[62] Specific types of expertise can even become a type of commodity, with groups selling their services to each other. Technical knowledge of such things as explosives, weaponry, suicide techniques and targeting have been shared among groups as disparate as Hizbullah, the LTTE, the Provisional IRA and the FARC.

Terrorism and criminality reflect the two dominions of authority of the modern nation-state: the internal legal dimension and the external strategic dimension. They are intertwined.[63] Nonetheless, there is a distinction between groups that engage primarily in attacks on non-combatants to achieve a political objective, and those that engage primarily in criminal activities to enrich themselves. Both can be brutal, and both may engage in the same types of behaviour, including kidnapping, assassinations and bombings, but their purposes are different. Terrorist groups are revisionist actors who want to alter the national or international political system in some way. Criminal syndicates aim to keep their activities out of view, and seek the perpetuation of the current political order so as to continue their illicit acts. Thus, criminal groups are status-quo actors, content to operate within the current system, which is the source of their riches, even as they distort it and transgress its laws and norms. Criminal behaviour is by no means good news, but when a group moves away from terrorism and towards criminality the challenge it presents can at least potentially be managed within existing legal frameworks. Moreover, criminal activities often harm the reputation of a revolutionary group within its actual or potential constituency, making its commitment to an ideology or cause seem shallow.

Terrorist campaigns may also develop in the direction of more conventional types of violence. Terrorism and insurgency overlap and are cousins, and the same organisations can use both methods, but they are different phenomena. Reviewing the twentieth-century record, the success rate for insurgencies (which attack military targets and typically shore up a constituency's support) has been higher than the success rate for terrorist organisations (which attack civilian or non-combatant targets and often undermine their own support). Terrorism is the *weak* tactic of the weak: used alone it rarely proves to be a winning approach over the long term. Being seen as an insurgency gives a campaign a degree of legitimacy: 'terrorist' is a pejorative term in a way that 'insurgent' is not. From the perspective of strategic counter-terrorism, a group gaining enough strength to move into an insurgency is a bad outcome.

There is yet another, even more sobering way that terrorist campaigns may transform: by acting as a catalyst for a conventional war. Terrorism on its own is a minor tactic; however, when it interacts with states it can potentially set off a cascade of actions that results in major, even systemic war. This outcome might occur if an attack is perceived to be sponsored by another state, prompting a retaliatory military action that escalates out of control, destabilises the local or regional power balance and leads to the perception that other states must protect themselves, or even pre-emptively attack. Clearly, the use of a weapon of mass destruction by a non-state group, particularly a nuclear or biological weapon, would dramatically increase the impact of an attack and the degree of international volatility that would follow – states would be strongly inclined to turn against each other following such an attack. As we have seen, such a constellation of circumstances (even without WMD) has occurred at least once in the past, when the murder of Archduke Franz Ferdinand set off a series of seemingly irreversible policy decisions that culminated in a war that left millions dead. In an age of preponderantly democratic states, whose greatest strength and greatest weakness is their tendency to be driven by the passions and energies of their people, the threat of this kind of cataclysm in the aftermath of a major terrorist attack is if anything greater than it has been at other periods in history.

Implications for counter-terrorism

The relevant question for policymakers in the midst of the current campaign is not 'how are we doing?', but rather 'how will it end?'. Believing that a conflict never ends is psychologically self-defeating: war is prolonged because we have no firm idea how to avoid classic mistakes and bring it to a close, and thus we do not put in place policies that are designed with an end in mind. But there is a great deal of experience with terrorist campaigns ending, either because of actions taken against them or because of dynamics of their own, frequently related to the vulnerable connection between groups and their constituents or audiences.

Concentrating on the six patterns discussed here, and determining which is most relevant to the current threat, is the best way to confound the short-term strategies of terrorism. While this cannot guarantee an outcome, knowledge of these long-standing patterns can enable leaders to see beyond the time-honoured and persistent tactics of terrorism. Above all else is the imperative to think beyond the passions of those who are hurt, frightened or angry. Policymakers who become caught up in the short-term goals and spectacle of terrorist attacks relinquish the broader historical perspective and phlegmatic approach that is crucial to the reassertion of state power. Their goal must be to think strategically and avoid falling into the trap of reacting narrowly and directly to the violent initiatives taken by these groups. Consciously driving a terrorist campaign towards its end is preferable to answering the tactical elements of a movement as it unfolds, and is also far more likely to result in success.

CHAPTER THREE

Ending Al-Qaeda

Al-Qaeda targets civilians to exploit vulnerabilities in Western civilisation so as to achieve its political ends. As has been the case throughout the modern history of terrorism, al-Qaeda is concerned with the weaknesses of the Western-style nation-state (particularly the United States), from which it draws its power. Terrorist attacks target the fabric of the state, ripping at a vulnerable seam between domestic law and foreign war, the internal and external realms of authority. The legal structure so essential to the nation-state has flaws that are being exploited, and Western strategy, with its preference for direct military action, also falls short in confronting this enemy. Over time, these political and legal structures must evolve, and so they will. But the best and only feasible way to adapt policies *now* and reverse the fortunes of al-Qaeda and its associates is to shift the emphasis away from the vulnerabilities and vanities of Western-style nation-states, and instead focus on the plentiful weaknesses of the foe.

Having examined the logic of terrorist strategy and developed a conceptual framework for how terrorist campaigns end, we now turn to the specific logic of al-Qaeda strategy, and explain how the framework provided here can be adapted to construct an effective counter-strategy for ending it. A strategy that draws on the most pertinent lessons from ending other terrorist groups can be devised to meet al-Qaeda's most potent threat, namely its ability to transcend borders and governments and mobilise people in a violent jihad.

The logic of al-Qaeda's strategy

The terrorist strategies of coercion and compellence, provocation, polarisation and mobilisation have all evolved concomitant with global changes in technology, patterns of transportation, communications, sources of wealth, cultural changes and political or ideological developments. Over time, there are relative shifts in the degree to which each of these strategies is employed, because they are not all equally successful within changing historical contexts, and groups that employ losing strategies do not long survive. But al-Qaeda has shown staying power. For reasons elaborated below, the most promising strategy within the present global milieu is one centred on mobilisation, and al-Qaeda's recognition of that fact is the most important reason why it has endured.

Provocation especially suited the nineteenth-century context because of the nature of the predominant political actors, especially in Europe. Aging autocratic states, with their sclerotic bureaucracies and anachronistic nobility, were keenly vulnerable to attacks calculated to further erode their legitimacy and expose the vacuous nature of their power. The French and American revolutions had demonstrated the supremacy of states founded on the passions and energies of the populace. Provoking the autocratic state to overreact served to deploy the regime's own strength against it, eliciting a reaction from the people and releasing these same explosive revolutionary forces.

Compellence best fitted the mid twentieth century because it aligned with nationalist movements whose aims could be expressed in terms of territory. It is no accident that terrorism was closely intertwined with insurgencies throughout the twentieth century. Colonial states under pressure for other reasons, especially in the immediate aftermath of the Second World War, were highly susceptible to coercion and compellence. As the decolonisation process unfolded and scores of new states gained recognition in the United Nations, the resources and sympathies of the global audience shifted steadily towards the cause of national self-determination. Colonial governments lost their legitimacy. Groups that used compellence as their guiding strategy often developed from terrorism to insurgency to independence, successfully establishing sovereign nation-states.

Polarisation was at the core of Marxist movements, and reached its apogee internationally in the interwar years with the struggle between communism and fascism for the soul of the nation-state. The defeat of fascist Japan and Germany resolved the question of whether states could find their legitimacy in the furtherance of an extreme ethnic nationalism. But the struggle between communism and capitalism continued throughout the Cold War, playing out domestically in the form of terrorism from the right and the left. The demise of the Soviet Union firmly answered this question as well, but more elemental issues of identity within modern states quickly filled the void. In the last years of the century, terrorist attacks designed to polarise societies along racial, religious, tribal, linguistic or ethnic lines regularly escalated into widespread and bloody civil wars.

In the context of sweeping changes in communications and economic ties, porous borders and dramatic cultural and political developments, the most powerful strategy of terrorism today is mobilisation. The twenty-first century is uniquely well suited to the use of terrorist attacks to marshal a following and draw attention to a cause. The democratisation of global communications has resulted in a concomitant democratisation of violence, including terrorist violence. The information revolution is not just changing the way people fight; it is altering the way people think and what they decide to fight *for*. In their enthusiasm for globalisation and the information age, the leaders of Western and Western-style nation-states have fallen behind in shaping (or even understanding) the narrative of the twenty-first century, currently an amalgam of unchecked market forces, resentment of globalisation, fear for the future of the planet and a search for spiritual meaning. The outcome of these global political shifts is difficult to predict.

Of the classic strategies of terrorism, therefore, al-Qaeda's most promising and effective has been mobilisation. Al-Qaeda's most potent sources of strength are its powerful image and carefully crafted narrative, assets constructed through widespread, well-developed and sophisticated efforts to build popular support for the cause. Although the group has a traditional, territorially based core, currently reconstituted in the frontier regions of Pakistan, this is not the source of its most serious long-term global threat. Al-Qaeda is at heart a brilliant propaganda and image machine whose primary purpose has been to convince Muslims that they can defeat the West and in this way solve their problems. Even as the group suffers military defeat after military defeat, al-Qaeda uses the actions and policies of the West to build an enraging and inspirational story designed to convince Muslims that they are honour-bound to defeat the West and thereby put an end to the humiliations, failures, frustrations, helplessness and deprivations that they have endured. This message is capturing the attention of young Muslims in many states, including in relatively privileged settings in the West, where clichés about terrorism arising out of deprivation or personal grievance may ring hollow. These young people are the new foot soldiers, mobilised, frequently in a kind of twenty-first-century cyber-conscription, to sacrifice themselves for their communities in the service of a new, pious political order. They see themselves as the new knights or epic heroes. The ability to reach and inspire this audience is the source of al-Qaeda's power and the engine of its strategy, thus far circumventing and confounding the actions of the United States and its allies, not least because of their engrained dyadic linear thinking.

Terrorism's strategic triad

In terrorism, strategy is not simply the application of means to ends, because the reaction of audiences to the violence can be a group's means, ends or both. Especially in the twenty-first century, terrorism cannot simply be considered within a dichotomous framework because the role of the audience is a third strategic factor that may well determine the outcome. And the audiences of concern are not just 'domestic' and 'international', as if terrorist groups were fledgling states. They are complex and varied and, for any given group, may include members of the group, potential members of the group, rival factions, passive supporters, active supporters, bystanders, potential targets and the target government.

Because of developments in communications, economics, social structures and political orders – globalisation, in a word – the nature of terrorism has evolved. The relative importance of the audience, always vital, has increased significantly in recent decades. War evolves as society evolves, and this applies equally to terrorism, another human enterprise. War has always been a part of the totality of human experience, and its character changes throughout history, reflecting changes in technology, economic systems, social structures, ideologies and political orders. As Michael Howard reminds us, war is inseparable from its broader historical context. Terrorism is not war, having more in common with crime, especially during the twentieth century. But terrorism *mimics* war in the sense that effective terrorist campaigns also have strategies that emerge out of and in turn affect the broader context within which they occur, and these strategies progress as society and the modern nation-state are transformed. Terrorist attacks are not the engines of change or expressions of policy that wars are, but they are signposts of changes, symbols of trends already under way that may catalyse or lead to systemic wars.

Groups employing terrorism are seeking to siphon sufficient power from the state to appeal to the third leg of terrorism's triad, the audiences which react to the violence and give it purchase. Some pathways of decline are under greater state control, others are related more to collective activity and the tendency of terrorist groups to implode, and some involve both.

But both state and non-state actors must be mindful of the third crucial element in the strategic equation. In the twenty-first century, the role of the audience is arguably more ubiquitous, more instantaneous, more powerful and more direct than ever before, and it is at the heart of the legitimacy of the Western-style nation-state. This is the main reason why strategies of compellence tend to falter and perpetuate, rather than end, terrorism.

Direct, instantaneous access to an empowered transnational audience is also why mobilisation is an especially powerful strategy for al-Qaeda. The al-Qaeda leadership grasps this strategic logic. Without global communication al-Qaeda would probably still be a local network, but it is neither ubiquitous nor immortal. The framework for understanding how terrorist campaigns end can offer insights into how to counter the group, and that is where we will turn next.

How might al-Qaeda end?

The historical framework for how terrorist campaigns end can give us insights into al-Qaeda's likely demise, although not all aspects are equally relevant. Analysis of the individual characteristics of a group, as well as the unique historical and political context within which it is operating, is vital. Al-Qaeda is not the same as many of its predecessors. It has an unusually flexible structure, boasts global reach, at times acts as a wealthy resource centre or operational facilitator and functions best as a propaganda focal point for a wider movement. While re-establishing old-fashioned facilities in the frontier provinces of Pakistan, its radicalisation and recruitment methods have unusual reach and sophistication. Al-Qaeda behaves more like a social movement than a classic terrorist group, especially as one moves further away from direct contact with the core. And, as mentioned, its use of the tools of globalisation, particularly contemporary means of communication, enables the rapid dissemination of its message and an instant connection to an audience. Al-Qaeda represents the next stage in the evolution of terrorism in the twenty-first century.

Because al-Qaeda has successfully exploited globalisation and crafted a virulent pseudo-religious philosophy, some Western analysts go so far as to reject comparisons with earlier groups, arguing that the current terrorist threat is unprecedented and that new modes of analysis are needed. Observers labelled Islamist groups the 'new terrorism' and rejected comparisons with historical predecessors, which they claimed reflected different aims, organisational structures, ideologies, types of attacks, potential lethality and goals, and hence were fundamentally discontinuous with al-Qaeda.[1] The attacks of 11 September 2001 seemed to confirm the looming threat, offering proof to many Americans that terrorism had developed from a peripheral nuisance into a major threat, a threat which sought massive casualties and access to so-called weapons of mass destruction. Critics also believed that the twentieth-century study of terrorism was too heavily biased towards Europe. If that was the 'old terrorism' then it was irrelevant: al-Qaeda was hardly the IRA with beards or the Red Brigades with suicide belts. This was an 'existential threat' that required fresh new thinking.

While the threat is indeed real and palpable, the extent of al-Qaeda's innovation has been exaggerated. Whereas changes in technology are worrying, the group itself consciously studies, analyses and builds upon historical predecessors, with which there is a long track record of experience. Memories are too short. For example, al-Qaeda has tentacular global reach and a mutable cell structure, but the socialist-anarchists of the late nineteenth century were comparable cell-based terrorist networks, whose attacks were likewise carried out by home-grown individuals 'inspired' by their philosophies and precedent. The al-Qaeda movement perpetuates itself by constructing an image of unity and uniqueness, tailoring its propaganda to different audiences, and many Western analysts are taken in by its rhetoric. But while innovative, al-Qaeda shares classic characteristics with earlier groups, particularly their vulnerabilities – as al-Qaeda analysts who pore over the lessons of their historical predecessors clearly realise. Al-Qaeda is dangerous, but it is neither unprecedented nor immortal.

Understanding the history of how terrorist groups end, particularly the six patterns of endings that have emerged from this analysis, gives us insight into how al-Qaeda is and is not likely to become extinct. First, it shares few characteristics with groups that have ended through decapitation of the leadership, all of whom have been hierarchically structured, reflected a cult of personality and lacked a viable successor. A scenario in which al-Qaeda is ended through the removal of bin Laden is difficult to imagine at this point. It is virtually impossible that he would be captured and held alive, not least because those around him have orders to kill him first. He would almost certainly be 'martyred'. His death would seriously damage the core leadership and reduce its effectiveness, but given the widespread dissemination of al-Qaeda's message in the past five years, this would not drive the movement towards its end.

As for military repression, the limits of such an approach have been amply demonstrated, especially when poorly coordinated with other measures. Democratic states have historically found it very difficult to sustain repression at home and abroad against terrorist groups, and this pattern is repeating itself. Because military or police action requires a target, the use of force against operatives works best in situations where members of the organisation can be separated from the surrounding population. This requires some kind of 'profiling' – always a sensitive issue, not least because the kind of discrimination required to prevent terrorist attacks virtually always relates to how members are defined (race, age, religion, nationality, etc.) rather than what they do (which by definition has not yet happened). Repressive measures carry with them high resource and opportunity costs and may undermine domestic support over time, further undercutting the state's ability to respond effectively to future terrorist attacks. Although the use of military force has demonstrated Western strength, prevented some attacks and eliminated members of the leadership, it is not driving al-Qaeda towards its end. Repression by *local* forces against foreign-inspired or foreign-supported terrorism, as by Sunnis in Anbar Province in Iraq, is an exception. Here, the use of force, occurring along local tribal lines, and has been successful in reducing the influence of foreign al-Qaeda fighters, at least in the short term. Beyond al-Qaeda and beyond terrorism, however, in Iraq the primary concern is a regionally destabilising civil war following the disengagement of American forces.

The third scenario, in which al-Qaeda ends after achieving its strategic objectives, clearly does not apply. In the most general terms, al-Qaeda's aims are to mobilise the umma to rise up, throw off the influence of the West (especially the United States), eliminate its support for corrupt Arab regimes and then install a pious order (sometimes referred to as a new Caliphate) that unites the 'Muslim world'. With the exception of its demonstrated success in mobilising many young Muslims, al-Qaeda is not approaching its stated strategic objectives; indeed, the West's response to its attacks has made them more unreachable than ever.[2] Al-Qaeda is achieving intermediate, tactical goals, such as increasing its international links and catching the attention of a wider audience of young Muslims, most notably in the West, accomplishments that are helping to perpetuate its violent campaign. But that is a far cry from achieving its strategic aims.

Likewise, the fourth scenario of a terrorist organisation's end – negotiations – seems impossible, as conceding al-Qaeda's demands would require overturning the international system as we currently understand it. However, we must be careful in how we use the term 'al-Qaeda'. Negotiations with local affiliates that have only recently joined the movement may be all but unavoidable. Many formerly nationalist groups are aligning themselves with al-Qaeda, and they may or may not share its broader aims. Al-Qaeda's ambitions are so sweeping that they are unlikely to comport with the specific local grievances of many groups that have recently pledged their allegiance, either formally or informally. Disaggregating the threat and weakening the movement requires understanding and enlarging its internal inconsistencies. This means dealing with local concerns on a local basis, considering priorities that may be irrelevant to or at odds with the Egyptian- and Saudi-dominated al-Qaeda leadership, and this may involve engaging in talks on a case-by-case basis.

Fifthly, al-Qaeda is not going to implode or lose its support in the usual way, by fading away between generations. It has already passed through a second, third and arguably fourth generation of operatives. But groups also end because the ideology becomes irrelevant, the group loses contact with 'the people', or mistaken targeting leads to a backlash by the group's constituency. As its key leaders regularly admit in their writings, all three of these are dangers for the al-Qaeda movement. The group is making a great many such errors, and is afflicted by deep-rooted factionalisation and infighting. Yet al-Qaeda's ample signs of disunity seem invisible to Western policymakers, many of whom are more focused on the domestic audience and unwisely name virtually every terrorist challenge 'al-Qaeda', thereby enhancing its image of power and unity. Reducing the group's public support would be best accomplished through highlighting the ample mistakes al-Qaeda is making, particularly in targeting Muslim civilians. In their failure to exploit al-Qaeda's serious mistakes of timing, targets and technique, the United States and its allies have missed a time-honoured method of ending a terrorist group (or enabling it to end itself). As will be further explained below, ending al-Qaeda by acting in a way that is synergistic with its own tendency towards marginalisation and implosion holds considerable promise for its opponents.

The final scenario, which sees al-Qaeda moving away from terrorism and towards full insurgency or, more worrying, catalysing all-out inter-state war, may be playing itself out before our eyes. Many analysts believe that al-Qaeda is already a global insurgency.[3] But calling it an insurgency only serves al-Qaeda's interests, as the group (like many terrorist groups) aspires to such a status and enjoys the enhanced legitimacy that such a label imparts. Moreover, al-Qaeda has already (intentionally or not) prompted two conventional wars whose full implications for stability in the 'Muslim world' and beyond have not yet fully emerged. While ending al-Qaeda is a top priority, terrorism is by no means the most dangerous threat facing the West: the end of terrorism is not necessarily the beginning of peace.

A strategy to end al-Qaeda: counter-mobilisation

By placing the logic of al-Qaeda's twenty-first century strategy within the framework of how other campaigns have met their demise, the United States and its allies can construct an effective counter-strategy for ending al-Qaeda. The major elements are as follows. Firstly, we must demystify the movement and clarify exactly what 'al-Qaeda' is, avoiding the unfortunate tendency to generalise and label everything that threatens us by that name. Secondly, we must understand and then exploit the cleavages that are present in the movement, thereby reducing its ability to act. Thirdly, we must disaggregate and hive off the constituent elements of al-Qaeda, aiming particularly at disparate elements that have recently attached themselves to the movement but actually hold divergent aims. Fourthly, we must highlight al-Qaeda's mistakes, especially targeting errors that kill Muslim non-combatants, the very people al-Qaeda claims to protect and represent. The corollary, of course, is that we must also stop making our own mistakes. Fifthly, we must encourage a popular backlash against al-Qaeda, constructing a sophisticated, widespread counter-mobilisation that will deprive it of support and push it towards its demise.

All of these steps will help to arrest the transition of the movement to its next generation, reducing its appeal to potential supporters by highlighting its hypocrisies and delegitimising the al-Qaeda image. Policies of indirect action will enable the United States and its allies to reduce the threat and, by employing their own strategies of leverage, work synergistically with the natural tendency of the movement to implode. These measures draw from three of the six ways in which terrorist groups have ended: implosion, negotiation or diplomacy and targeted military force or repression. We will call this tailored strategy 'counter-mobilisation', because it works against al-Qaeda's strongest weapon.

Articulating 'al-Qaeda'

The first prong of a successful strategy to counter al-Qaeda's terrorism is to clarify to audiences around the globe exactly what al-Qaeda is and what it is not. This is not just of academic interest. It is partly because there is so much vague use of the name 'al-Qaeda' that it seems superhuman and ubiquitous. Groups that use terrorism rely upon psychological elements of warfare more heavily than others. When politicians and experts employ the term 'al-Qaeda' loosely, they help its propagandists to construct and perpetuate their desired image and to mobilise support. They also put in place a mental framework for an undifferentiated counter-terrorism policy that cannot possibly be effective against it.

The United States and its allies must mobilise a broad range of global audiences to attack elements of this threat, but they cannot target a vague monolith that they do not understand. Since the attacks of 2001, al-Qaeda has comprised three main elements: a core central group of leaders and strategists directly associated with bin Laden and Zawahiri; a nebula of more traditional groups that are formally or informally aligned with the core and sometimes respond to central guidance (often called the 'network'); and localised factions (even individuals) that have no physical contact with the centre, but strive to associate themselves with the worldview of al-Qaeda and its vaunted label.[4] This last element is particularly troublesome: some militants are called 'al-Qaeda' either because they trumpet the name or because skittish politicians do, but they are *not* formally aligned. Western leaders and terrorism analysts calling every localised plot by this name only perpetuates the myth. And that is fully intended by members: one training videotape instructs sympathisers to make false claims of responsibility in the wake of actions throughout the world, so as to further the movement.[5] It is no accident that the understanding of 'al-Qaeda' in the West is generally so poor.

The leadership of al-Qaeda consciously targets its messages to a wide and varied range of listeners. The discourse of bin Laden and Zawahiri contains elements of many other ideologies, including anti-imperialism, anti-globalisation, anti-Americanism, anti-Westernisation and anti-modernisation.[6] They tap into the wellspring of anger, frustration, humiliation and resentment that has built up over the decades of political Islam's failure, especially in states such as Saudi Arabia, Egypt and Pakistan, but also among displaced students and young second- and third-generation Muslim immigrants in the West.[7] This anger is brilliantly channelled by al-Qaeda through its discourse about the overthrow of 'apostate' governments, the Israeli–Palestinian conflict, the wars in Iraq and Afghanistan, the presence of Western troops in the holy territories, the emptiness of Western materialism and so forth. The group points to a conspiracy between Christendom and Judaism to destroy Islam, setting up a Manichean struggle between the US and its allies on the one hand, and the global Muslim community, the umma, on the other.[8]

Al-Qaeda is not the voice of 'The Muslim World', or even a major portion of it. In their pronouncements, bin Laden and Zawahiri try to act like leaders of an emerging pseudo-state, addressing the umma as if it belonged to them – a hollow fantasy that is further perpetuated by the West's tendency to hyperbolise its rhetoric in return. Al-Qaeda represents a powerful Salafist ideology, but its extreme anti-modern fundamentalism is adhered to by only a minority of Sunnis, and is hated by most Shi'ites and Sufis. What would an al-Qaeda future mean for them? Apart from negative messages, the specific picture of what al-Qaeda would *replace* current international circumstances with is deliberately vague. There is much evocative language, general references to restoring peace, instituting Islamic law, returning to an 'authentic' version of Islam and installing a modern Caliphate – a hazy dream of a better, more just future, to be achieved through a defensive jihad. But what exactly would that new Islamic 'state' or entity look like? This is not specified by the leadership, because doing so would undermine the movement itself.

Al-Qaeda is not 'an ideology'. As is obvious in the bitter doctrinal disputes among jihadists (many of which are accessible on the web), this is a complex movement packed with discord about what it stands for and what it aspires to be. But calling al-Qaeda 'an ideology', as some in the West do, is unhelpful from a counter-terrorism perspective.[9] In his book *Knights Under the Prophet's Banner*, Zawahiri calls the fight with the West a 'battle of ideologies, a struggle for survival, and a war with no truce'.[10] In a sense he is correct, as there is of course a huge difference between Western liberalism and the ideas represented by the al-Qaeda movement. But the front-lines of this fight lie within Islam. Zawahiri might *like* this to be a 'battle of ideologies', but it is primarily a battle over the ideology that should prevail among Muslims, and always has been. Nor is it by any means the first such battle that has occurred within the faith. Al-Qaeda is just one in a long line of radical splinter groups that has appeared in Islam.[11] Many of those who believe in what is loosely referred to as a 'global jihad', for example, differ in what they mean by that, whom they are willing to target, what their overall aims are in pursuing it and what the world will look like after they are finished. Their rhetoric is violent and nihilistic. There is ample evidence of disagreement in the fractious debates amongst them, virtually always with greater agreement about what they are *against* than what they are *for*.

Al-Qaeda is not a monolithic global movement. Western policies have lumped together many disparate groups that have engaged in terrorism, increasing their incentives to align against the West and provide support to al-Qaeda. The tactic of terrorism is despicable under all circumstances. But by failing to differentiate between the aims and constituencies of groups that have used terrorism (such as, for instance, the Shia Arab Hizbullah, the Islamist Hamas and the secular Palestinian Fatah), the West is failing to scrutinise and divide its enemies.[12] Many of the groups formally aligned with al-Qaeda are far more interested in local political aims than they are in the rhetoric of the movement. There are vast differences in the motivations, worldviews, tactics and aims of groups such as the Bangladeshi Jihad Movement, the Philippine Abu Sayyaf Group, the Eastern Turkistan Islamist Movement in the Xinjiang–Uighur autonomous region of China, the Libyan Islamic Fighting Group and the Pakistan-based Lashkar-e-Tayiba, for example, all of whom have some association with al-Qaeda. Those who have most recently (since 2005) professed their loyalty to bin Laden, including Allah's Brigade (Palestine), Al-Qaeda Maghreb Commandment (Morocco) and the Brigades of Kurdistan (Iraq), are particularly drawn to the power of the 'brand name', but differ in their specific local aims.[13]

For Western governments to gloss over these differences is a mistake.[14] In many circumstances, there is a strong argument against even using the name al-Qaeda. The term evokes an image that serves the movement, making it appear unified when it is not. The name itself evolved serendipitously, as even those within the movement point out. 'Abd Allah b. Nasir al-Rashid, an important jihadist ideologue, strategist and operations planner, wrote in a 2003 online article that the term 'al-Qaeda' was too restrictive, as it refers to the former regime in Afghanistan and specifically to bin Laden, whereas 'mujahadeen', the term al-Rashid advocates, appears in the Koran, evokes sacred Islamic history and encompasses more Islamic activists.[15] The fact that al-Rashid is moved to argue for a more inclusive, universalist name reflects the unease among some participants about the mythology of bin Laden and his cronies, especially the efforts of the centre to project an element of ideological and operational deference to al-Qaeda.[16] Again, unity is *not* what this movement represents.

In this era of globalised and instantaneous communications, how we refer to this threat matters because it suggests a narrative that guides and describes our efforts. Calling the al-Qaeda movement 'jihadi international', as the Israeli intelligence services do for example, encourages the kind of grouping together of disparate threats that undermines counterterrorism.[17] It is exactly the same mistake the West made in lumping the Chinese and the Soviets together in the 1950s and early 1960s under the label 'international communists'. It was only after we began to understand the crucial differences between them, including their divisive doctrinal disputes, divergent national interests and competing ambitions, that an effective response became possible that took advantage of these points of leverage. If the West makes the same mistake with al-Qaeda it will again fail to respond effectively, and will give other factions every incentive to draw together more closely.

The broader al-Qaeda's reach, the more the weaknesses and disparities in its vision emerge. This is not a very agile movement, intellectually: its leaders are unable to construct a positive image of the future, a narrative that moves beyond anger and violence, a future that would really appeal to a broad cross-section of the umma. A truly effective counter-strategy would critique al-Qaeda's 'platform' more rigorously and highlight the emptiness it offers modern Muslims. Western-style nation-states may be imperfect, impious, materialistic or culturally insensitive, and some of their recent policies may be debatable, unjust or even woefully misguided. The West must do better. But the *real* question to be tackled is: what precisely does al-Qaeda offer modern Muslims instead?

Exploiting internal cleavages
Violent internal cleavages and bickering are endemic to the al-Qaeda movement, and have been from the outset, and the second prong in a successful strategy against al-Qaeda is consciously to exploit them. Al-Qaeda's most effective means of papering over internal differences has been to tap into anger over perceived anti-Muslim violence in Chechnya, Bosnia, Afghanistan, Iraq, the Palestinian territories and elsewhere. But the infighting and factionalisation that was so apparent in the declining months of predecessors such as the Italian and German left-wing groups, the Provisional IRA, the FLQ, Combat-18 and the Abu Nidal Organisation is amply apparent in this movement, and al-Qaeda should be encouraged towards the same fate.

In the 1980s, tribal and national divisions among the mujahadeen were an impediment in fighting the Soviets in Afghanistan. Some 35,000 Muslim radicals from 43 different nations came to Afghanistan to fight.[18] Divided by their diverse languages, nationalities, customs, habits and to some degree beliefs, they were best able to align against a common foe. The Wahhabist practices of some of the Arab fighters also offended the Afghans, who saw them as unwelcome aliens. Bin Laden spoke despairingly of their *fitna*, or division and faction, which the Prophet Mohammed had expressly forbidden but which dogged the fighters. As soon as the atheist Soviets had gone, the mujahadeen fell again into bickering factionalism, with Afghan tribes seeking control over the country and the 'Arab-Afghans' – Egyptians, Algerians, Yemenis, Sudanese, Saudis, Tajiks, Uzbeks and others – refocused on the priorities of their own homelands.[19] These divisions have not gone away, although they are now subsumed under al-Qaeda's global anti-West 'jihad' rhetoric.[20]

Al-Qaeda cannot abide dissent, as it has at its heart a firm belief in the clarity of a single Salafist interpretation of Islam, as well as a strong distaste for anything that smacks of democratic pluralism.[21] Doctrinal disputes among key jihadi thinkers reveal crucial differences of opinion among senior members, even those of the same nationality. One long-standing source of dispute, for example, is between those who adhere to the beliefs of revered Salafist and Hadith scholar Shaikh al-Albani, who argues that jihad should entail some elements of compromise, and those who, like Zawahiri, argue that anything less than the killing of infidels is 'appeasement'.[22] Another element of discord is the issue of whether it is acceptable to kill Muslims, particularly women, children and the elderly. This theme appears over and over again, usually in the form of criticism levelled at al-Qaeda operatives after specific attacks. The usual response is that the violence is religiously sanctioned and necessary, and blame can be laid at the feet of Israel and the West.[23] But the regular and repeated defensiveness of al-Qaeda strategists about actions against innocent Muslims reveals an obvious sensitivity and source of vulnerability.

The United States and its allies seem oddly blind to opportunities to exploit these cleavages, even unwilling to take the time to understand them. For example, in November 2007, when the legendary Egyptian jihadist thinker Dr Sayyid Imam al-Sharif released a book renouncing his prior commitment to violence, the United States and its allies did next to nothing. One of Zawahiri's oldest associates, al-Sharif had been a major figure in the al-Qaeda movement. His earlier book, *Al-'Umda fi l'dad Al-'Udda* ('The Essentials of Making Ready [for Jihad]') was used in al-Qaeda training camps in Afghanistan. His 2007 book was written in a prison cell, prompting Zawahiri to mock him and question its authenticity, but nonetheless it represented an opportunity to broaden the differences among followers of al-Qaeda on the question of the legitimacy of violence. For example, the book argues that bin Laden is wrong to compare the actions of the 11 September operatives to the early raids of the Ansar warriors in the seventh to ninth centuries. The renunciation was released in a serialised format in the Egyptian daily newspaper *Al-Masry al-Youm* and the Kuwaiti newspaper *Al-Jarida* in November and December 2007, striking a blow against the narrative of the al-Qaeda movement, but little has been said about it in the West.[24]

There is a plethora of other long-standing tensions. These include whether it is right to call other Muslims 'apostates', to attack the economy of Muslim states (especially the tourism and oil industries), or to create political and social disorder.[25] The wisdom of targeting the United States rather than local governments continues to vex some members. Sectarian disputes are common, and not just in Iraq: in captured training video-tapes, Abu Musab Al Suri, architect of the flat hierarchical structure and 'individual terrorism' of al-Qaeda's post-2001 periphery, spurns any form of cooperation between Shi'ites and Sunnis, arguing that Shia groups like Hizbullah have had a negative influence on the Palestinians.[26] These debates are openly and easily accessible, especially on the Internet, but also in other media.[27] Even for those who only speak English, captured al-Qaeda documents have been translated and posted on the web, notably by the Counterterrorism Center at West Point, New York.[28] Such deep divisions and ideological inconsistencies could easily undermine al-Qaeda were the spotlight turned away from the unifying theme of the external threat to Islam, to highlight the movement itself.

Hiving off constituents

The third element in a successful strategy against al-Qaeda is to disaggre-gate the many elements of the movement and develop more sophisticated, targeted counter-terrorism policies tailored to its constituent parts. The aim must be to enlarge the movement's internal inconsistencies and differ-ences, to suggest a path towards a promising future that may be reached without engaging in Islamist violence. There is more hope of ending such groups through traditional methods if they are dealt with using traditional tools, potentially including economic aid, political concessions or negotia-tions with specific local elements that may have negotiable terms (albeit pursued through an illegitimate tactic).

While negotiations with al-Qaeda's core are impossible, many groups in the 'network' are only loosely connected, and the West's overall strate-gic interest lies in making distinctions among them and hiving them off. The conditions for negotiations on local issues must be evaluated on a case-by-case basis. The nihilistic goals of the al-Qaeda movement are distinct from the nationalist aspirations of many of the groups that are now to some degree aligning with it. In other contexts, successful Western-backed multi-party negotiations with local Islamic groups such as the Philippine Moro Islamic Liberation Front (MILF) or some of the more moderate Kashmiri separatist groups have demonstrated a willingness to consider the griev-ances of Muslim organisations on their own local terms, undermining the message of a dichotomous struggle between 'Islam' and 'the West'. This is not to say that a given al-Qaeda-affiliated group's aims are necessarily right, or that their tactics are legitimate (they are certainly not), only that the exten-sive local variation in groups and goals is being glossed over by the United States' obsession with the 'war on terror' and a monolithic 'al-Qaeda'.

In selected cases, this might also mean offering an exit to individual, peripheral members of al-Qaeda. Although amnesties for the core leadership and its closely aligned groups are obviously impossible, providing a way out for individuals who do not support all of the movement's more rigid tenets would be prudent.[29] Not everyone in the movement wants to be a suicide attacker. Given an honourable alternative to death, disgruntled individuals might choose to move against other members of the movement, leading to better intelligence and the undermining of some local cells.[30] Alternatively, whole groups that are more interested in nationalist objectives than in al-Qaeda's transnational, nihilist ideology might shift their allegiances and tactics. Even if these tactics are unrealistic for elements of al-Qaeda (whose ideology is admittedly more extreme than that of many of its predecessors), merely devising and announcing a potential avenue of escape might sow distrust among members, especially in al-Qaeda's periphery, and increase the resources necessary to vet new participants. Treating captured operatives extraordinarily *well*, for example, publicising their handling and perhaps even releasing them back to their cells, might be an effective way to undermine trust within the group.[31] As was the case with the Second of June Movement, other members might then turn upon them and engage in fratricide.

Universal prescriptions are impossible and ill advised, because al-Qaeda's affiliates in different regions use different methods and represent different local interests. But tactics to exploit them must become more nuanced, well informed and agile. In Europe, for example, subversive networks penetrate Muslim community organisations, mosques and youth groups, opportunistically exploiting local grievances such as the French headscarf ban and European countries' participation in Iraq and Afghanistan. As Australian army officer David Kilcullen points out, these networks infiltrate 'micro-havens' – urban undergrounds, alienated ethnic groups and slums – and exploit loopholes in European human-rights legislation to recruit young people to terrorist activity.[32] They may be even more threatening to local community institutions than they are to European governments. Responding to these networks requires an element of sophisticated counter-subversion, emphasising trusted networks and applying what Kilcullen terms 'integrated counterorganization, counter-motivation, countersanctuary, and counterideology measures'.[33]

Spotlighting al-Qaeda's mistakes

A fourth important prong in any successful strategy against the al-Qaeda leadership is to use their mistakes against them. Al-Qaeda has made a large number of serious targeting errors that have killed Muslims and have been decried by many in its own constituency, yet the West has not effectively publicised or capitalised on them. The United States tends to act as if al-Qaeda is essentially a static enemy that will react to its actions, but then fails to react effectively and strategically to the movement's missteps. As the Real IRA case demonstrates, the al-Qaeda movement can undermine itself if it is enabled to.

A prominent example of mistaken targeting that Zawahiri himself recounts in *Knights Under the Prophet's Banner* concerns the fate of a young girl called Shayma Abdel-Halim, who was killed in an attack on the motorcade of Egyptian Prime Minister Atef Sidqi by Zawahiri's own group, Islamic Jihad, in 1993.[34] The minister was only slightly injured, but Shayma, who was standing nearby in her schoolyard, was crushed by a door blown off his car by the explosion. As Lawrence Wright describes, Shayma's death so outraged the Egyptian population, who had seen more than 240 people killed by terrorist attacks during the previous two years, that they took to the streets, shouting 'Terrorism is the enemy of God!'. The crackdown and arrests that followed gutted almost the entire structure of Islamic Jihad, particularly when a computer belonging to the membership director was recovered, containing the entire database of members' names, addresses, houses where they might be hiding and even aliases.[35] Virtually the entire operation in Egypt was destroyed. It is no wonder that Zawahiri is keenly aware of the dangers of poor targeting and popular backlash.

Al-Qaeda itself assumed its current form in the course of regrouping after the 1997 Luxor attacks. The widespread revulsion that followed led Zawahiri to join bin Laden and announce the formation in 1998 of the Islamic Front for Jihad Against Jews and Crusaders, the coalition that formed the backbone of al-Qaeda. Senior members of the organisation are likewise cognisant of the dangers of engaging in the kind of convulsive, indiscriminate violence that engulfed the GIA in Algeria in the 1990s. Yet al-Qaeda, or groups claiming association with it, have staged numerous attacks that have resulted in carnage not only among so-called 'infidels' but also among Muslims, including women and children: the October 2002 attacks in Bali,[36] the May 2003 attacks in Saudi Arabia,[37] attacks in Istanbul in November 2003,[38] the 2004 Madrid bombings[39] and the London attacks of July 2005 all resulted in Muslim casualties, and outraged members of the Muslim community. The majority of the casualties in a series of simultaneous attacks in Casablanca, Morocco, in May 2003 were Muslims, as were *all* of the casualties in bomb attacks in Riyadh, Saudi Arabia, on 8 November 2003.[40] An attack on a hotel in the Jordanian capital Amman on 9 November 2005, orchestrated by al-Qaeda in Mesopotamia, killed 38 members of a Muslim wedding party, including parents of the bride and the groom, as well as Jordanians, Palestinians and Iraqis.[41]

In a widely reported letter captured in 2005, Zawahiri sharply criticised the late Abu Musab al-Zarqawi for his brutal attacks on Iraqi Shi'ites and the videotaped beheadings that disgusted ordinary Muslims:

> Many of your Muslim admirers among the common folk are wondering about your attacks on the Shia. The sharpness of this questioning increases when the attacks are on one of their mosques ... Among the things which the feelings of the Muslim populace who love and support you will never find palatable – also – are the scenes of slaughtering the hostages. You shouldn't be deceived by the praise of some of the zealous young men and their description of you as the shaykh of the slaughterers, etc. They do not express the general view.[42]

Zawahiri concludes by stressing that 'we are in a battle, and ... more than half of this battle is taking place in the battlefield of the media ... We don't need this.'[43]

It is clearly in the interests of those who oppose al-Qaeda to highlight its direct and indirect responsibility for attacks launched in its name that offend and hurt Muslims. The disadvantage of any wide-ranging, global movement is that its leaders do not have operational control over all elements. The very ubiquity of its reputation and influence make al-Qaeda responsible for a range of actions taken in its name, whether it approves of them or not. Such loss of operational control is a long-standing problem for many well-established groups, and the repercussions of damaging attacks have been a serious threat to the viability of many organisations: as we have seen, during the twentieth century this facilitated the implosion of terrorist groups as disparate as the UVF and the Red Brigades. Admittedly, al-Qaeda has never aspired to have full operational control over its elements; it arose from a desire to mobilise the masses in a widespread, self-generating uprising to, in al-Qaeda's terms, 'protect the umma from oppression'. It was meant to be a resource and catalyst, not a military hierarchy. Yet actions taken in its name do not always advance its agenda.

The attitudes of Muslim and Western publics are increasingly converging, yet the West focuses on itself and does little to nurture cooperation. There is a growing sense of outrage about the killing of non-combatants – on vacation, attending weddings, at the market, on their way to work or school, many of them deeply religious and a large proportion of whom also happen to be Muslim. If the United States and its allies fail to grasp this opportunity, to work with local cultures and local people to build upon common goals and increase their alienation from al-Qaeda, then they will have missed a long-established and promising technique for ending it.

Facilitating the backlash

Support for al-Qaeda is eroding, and the fifth element in a Western strategy to end al-Qaeda is to further facilitate this process, not least by avoiding further mistakes. A backlash among Muslims against terrorism is well under way.[44] Views of the leadership itself are also becoming more negative: for example, in 2003 more than 50% of Jordanians said that they believed bin Laden would 'do the right thing'; by 2007, the figure was only 20%.[45] There are many anecdotal examples of a popular backlash in the wake of attacks associated with or inspired by al-Qaeda. For example, following the May 2003 Casablanca attacks, there was a protest march, public support for local Islamists dropped precipitously and the government moved towards greater cooperation with the United States and France. The sole legal Islamist party in Morocco, the Party of Justice and Development, was roundly defeated in the elections that took place shortly after the attacks.[46] Following the al-Qaeda attacks in Riyadh in 2003, there was widespread anger and a ferocious dispute online, with many participants arguing that the attacks were illegitimate. Similar controversy erupted following the 2005 London bombings, including a widely read fatwa issued by Abu Basir, a Syrian Islamist scholar living in London. Abu Basir argued that he supported jihad but not the idea of revenge. There are countless other examples.

Muslims are paying the heaviest price for al-Qaeda's campaign, and this hypocrisy should be more widely publicised. One of the main stated objectives of al-Qaeda is to pressure the United States to stop supporting or carrying out military invasions that kill Muslims around the world, including in Chechnya, Bosnia, Timor Leste, Israel and Iraq.[47] How can it make sense that al-Qaeda's attacks also result in scores of Muslim deaths? The concept of Islam under attack and on the defensive is at the very core of the justification of mass-casualty terrorism, and it is a consistent theme through doctrinal debates on the Internet, over the air-waves and in pamphlets, books, cassette tapes and sermons. But the degree to which al-Qaeda has sponsored (or been associated with) attacks that have themselves killed large numbers of Muslims throughout the world – particularly children, women and old men – is not widely publicised.[48]

Although it is difficult to determine precisely the number of Muslims who have died in al-Qaeda attacks (casualties are generally not tallied according to religion), carefully examining available evidence yields the conclusion that at least 40% of the victims have been Muslims – and this in operations that were specifically designed as a symbolic protest against Muslim oppression.[49] This figure only includes attacks for which al-Qaeda has claimed direct responsibility, and Chechnya-related violence is excluded. If the full range of attacks inspired by or tied to al-Qaeda were included, the proportion of Muslim victims would be even higher. And what exactly has been accomplished with all of these deaths? Held up to the light, al-Qaeda's strategy is ultimately self-defeating: it is killing the very people on whose behalf it claims to be acting.

Beyond al-Qaeda

Al-Qaeda is dangerous, and Western nation-states must counter it with vigorous actions that strive to eliminate the core leadership and protect their own people. The argument here is by no means a call for passivity or complacency, as inaction against this threat invites trouble as easily as action at times exacerbates it: al-Qaeda can still kill a great many people. Instead, the argument here is to envision the end of al-Qaeda as a means of shifting the focus away from tactics and towards a long-term strategy that will end in victory. In ending this group, some actions are more effective than others, because they have a multiplying effect and have the potential to push al-Qaeda towards its own implosion and demise. The number of mistakes the West is making must be reduced, and policymakers must dig more deeply into an analysis of this threat. Al-Qaeda can be targeted by employing strategies of leverage that take advantage of the movement's vulnerabilities and its natural propensity to decline and fail, but this will require intelligence and patience.

The sad truth of the human condition is that violence both attracts and repels, having an impact upon observers whose motivations and sympathies may be complex and contradictory. But over time it mainly repels, especially when it is directed against the most helpless and illegitimate targets, as terrorist attacks by definition are. In the end, human beings are left with the question of how to protect what they value and move forwards to a better future. What that future might look like is a question al-Qaeda is not answering. There is no positive vision beyond the violence and carnage that offer an outlet for humiliation and rage, but little more.

A Post Al-Qaeda World

The history of how terrorist groups end leads to the conclusion that the most effective way to push al-Qaeda's campaign to its finish is to employ policies that highlight the flaws of the movement itself and the illegitimacy of its actions, using strategies of leverage that counter and exceed those that it is using itself. The flaws of al-Qaeda are appalling: indiscriminate killing in the service of a largely fictitious narrative without a shred of hopeful vision. That al-Qaeda has achieved mass mobilisation of recruits and supporters is a product of globalisation, and a counter-mobilisation strategy must seek to find purchase or leverage against al-Qaeda's very heart.

The strategies of terrorism emerge in and reflect unique historical, political and social contexts that are constantly evolving. Nonetheless, long-standing experience with groups that use terrorism demonstrates that they invariably end, and do so according to certain patterns. Among the six pathways described here, at least three yield insights into a strategy for defeating al-Qaeda. By combining elements of targeted force with techniques for hastening implosion and fragmentation, a hybrid indirect and more effective strategy of counter-mobilisation can be erected.

Western-style nation-states are intimately familiar with indirect strategies of leverage, even if their leaders tend to be geopolitical amnesiacs. Their impact and effectiveness is best understood in retrospect, when reviewing the dynamics of terrorist campaigns during their last months. Studying the endings of campaigns brings the strategic question into relief, like an autopsy that dissects the dynamics of a disease process and reveals how to alter it in the future. Understanding the logic of terrorism offers ample lessons for al-Qaeda's demise. The most promising policy avenues transcend the dichotomous strategic-studies framework that locks us into dysfunctional debates, and instead relate to the nature of the al-Qaeda movement itself, its flaws and the illegitimacy of its actions. In other words, we must minimise the ability of the movement to draw power from the state, and aggressively and synergistically amplify al-Qaeda's natural tendency to end itself.

Three fundamental lessons for policymakers emerge from careful study of al-Qaeda and its predecessors. Firstly, understand the well-established strategies of terrorism as they have evolved throughout history. Do not assume that the purpose of a terrorist campaign is coercion, because these campaigns are above all opportunistic and exploit the circumstances within which they operate. In the current context, all of the strategies of terrorism are being employed, but the most effective has been direct, widespread mobilisation of a following through the technologies of globalisation. Secondly, the most effective way to drive a group towards its end is to leverage its mistakes, as the group leverages the mistakes of the government it opposes. The corollary is, of course, that the government must minimise the mistakes that groups such as al-Qaeda take advantage of, for it is from the errors of the state that such groups draw their best fuel. Finally, in fighting al-Qaeda policymakers must remember to keep their psychological framework out of the tactical dynamic of terrorism and counter-terrorism, for that is the realm in which groups have the best chance of perpetuating themselves and achieving their objectives. It is much more effective for governments to take a strategic perspective that consciously drives towards a realistic image of the end of the campaign.

NOTES

Introduction

1   The author would like to thank John Wooding, Hanna Ucko and Carolina Johnson for their help in completing this monograph, and is also grateful to Patrick M. Cronin, Hew Strachan and Adam Roberts for their support. The author alone is responsible for any remaining flaws.

2   B.H. Liddell Hart, *Strategy* (London: Faber and Faber, 1954; reprinted by Penguin Books, 1991), p. 322.

3   For states, 'strategy' means the application of military means to fulfil the ends of policy. Using the word to refer to the activities of a non-state actor is unconventional. However, groups that use the violent tactic of terrorism as a means to accomplish long-term political ends may be said to be devising a form of strategy. That is the sense in which the word is employed here. See Hew Strachan, 'The Lost Meaning of Strategy', *Survival*, vol. 47, no. 3, Autumn 2005, pp. 33–54.

Chapter One

1   'Terrorist group' means a non-state group that uses the tactic of terrorism – or the threat or use of violence against non-combatants or civilians – to accomplish its political aims. Some states also use state organs for the purpose of inspiring terror, whether against their own citizens or internationally. Indeed, over the course of the centuries, in wars, conflicts and brutal domestic crackdowns, states have been responsible for far more violence against civilians, including crimes against humanity, violations of the laws of war and genocide. But state violence is not the main focus of this paper.

2   There may be parallels between the decisions made by terrorist leaders and those made by state governments. Overwhelming evidence indicates that, while it is an illegitimate tactic, terrorism is carried out by rational human beings who calculate the costs and benefits of attacks. See, for example, Martha Crenshaw, 'The Logic of Terrorism: Terrorist Behavior as a Product of Strategic Choice', in Walter Reich (ed.), *Origins of Terrorism: Psychologies, Ideologies, Theologies, States*

of Mind (Washington DC: The Woodrow Wilson Center Press, 1998), pp. 7–24.

3 I explain the historical dimension of terrorism's evolution in more depth in 'Behind the Curve: Globalization and International Terrorism', *International Security*, vol. 27, no. 3, Winter 2002–2003, pp. 30–58.

4 Thomas Schelling's concept of 'coercion' is the use or threat of force. As further developed in the writings of Alexander George, coercion involves positive incentives, such as diplomacy, as well as negative actions that hurt the target government. Lawrence Freedman also argues that strategic coercion may involve deterrence. Because non-state actors do not have the full range of positive and negative incentives available to states, compellence – a subset of coercion which means the use of threats to influence another actor to stop an unwanted behaviour or to start doing something a group wants it to do – more precisely describes what terrorism tries to accomplish. Thomas Schelling, *Arms and Influence* (New Haven, CT: Yale University Press, 1966); Alexander L. George and William E. Simons (eds), *The Limits of Coercive Diplomacy*, revised edition (Boulder, CO: Westview Press, 1994); and Lawrence Freedman, *Strategic Coercion: Concepts and Cases* (New York: Oxford University Press, 1998), fn. 1, p. 326.

5 See, for example, Juliet Lodge, *Terrorism: A Challenge to the State* (London: St Martin's Press, 1981).

6 This kind of thinking also removes the imperative to grapple with the divergent strategic thinking and worldview of the attacker. A Western economic model of two 'rational' actors is enough.

7 For figures, see Audrey Kurth Cronin, 'Rethinking Sovereignty: American Strategy in the Age of Terrorism', *Survival*, vol. 44, no. 2, Summer 2002, pp. 119–39.

8 An argument about the effectiveness of terrorism as a strategy of attrition, particularly forcing states to withdraw from territory, is provided by Andrew H. Kydd and Barbara F. Walter, 'The Strategies of Terrorism', *International Security*, vol. 31, no. 1, Summer 2006, pp. 49–80. In addition to the strategies mentioned here, Kydd and Walter include spoiling and outbidding. But spoiling applies only to specific situations such as negotiations, and outbidding refers only to competition between rival terrorist groups. Both are tactics (or process goals); neither directly addresses a campaign's overall purpose (or outcome goals). See the argument in my forthcoming *How Terrorism Ends*, Chapter 3.

9 See for example Daniel G. Arce and Todd Sandler, 'Terrorist Signalling and the Value of Intelligence', *British Journal of Political Science*, vol. 37, no. 4, October 2007, pp. 573–86.

10 But states are just as likely to respond by redoubling their efforts, as the Russians did in Chechnya and the Indians did in Kashmir.

11 If the main target of attacks were the US military in Iraq, this argument would be more convincing. The overwhelming tendency to kill Iraqi security forces and Iraqi civilians does not support it, and most of the suicide attackers are not Iraqi. See Mohammed M. Hafez, *Suicide Bombers in Iraq: The Strategy and Ideology of Martyrdom* (Washington DC: US Institute of Peace Press, 2007), especially pp. 214–15.

12 By incorporating both combatants and non-combatants into what he calls 'suicide terrorism', Pape departs from the widespread practice that designates terrorism as an illegitimate tactic primarily because it targets non-combatants. Many operations target military forces and are therefore guerrilla or insurgent operations. It is no wonder that Pape concludes that their purpose is to force a military operation to end. The commonality in the attacks he studies is the suicide of the operative, not the use of terrorism. Robert A. Pape, *Dying To Win: The Strategic Logic of Suicide Terrorism* (New York: Random House, 2005).

13 *Ibid.*, p. 30.

14 This argument builds on the excellent overview of terrorism's strategies provided by Martha Crenshaw, 'Terrorism and Global Security', in Chester A. Crocker, Fen Osler Hampson and Pamela Aall (eds), *Leashing the Dogs of War: Conflict Management in a Divided World* (Washington DC: US Institute of Peace Press, 2007), pp. 73–5.

15 Walter Laqueur calls Heinzen's *Der Mord* ('Murder') 'the most important ideological statement of early terrorism'. The quote is from Heinzen's *Der Mord* as reproduced in Walter Laqueur (ed.), *Voices of Terror* (New York: Reed Press, 2004), p. 50.

16 Serge Stepniak-Kravchinski, *Underground Russia* (London, 1883), reprinted in *Voices of Terror*, p. 93.

17 Joseph Conrad, *The Secret Agent* (London: Penguin Classics, 2007), p. 268.

18 On Princip's naiveté, see Adam Roberts, 'The "War on Terror" in Historical Perspective', *Survival*, vol. 47, no. 2, Summer 2005, p. 107.

19 The Black-and-Tans who fought the Irish revolutionaries in the early twentieth century are another example. Their methods were effective, but brutal. See David Fromkin, 'The Strategy of Terrorism', *Foreign Affairs*, vol. 53, no. 4, July 1975, pp. 686–7. One of the best known twentieth-century theorists of efforts to provoke the state into repression is Carlos Marighella, whose *Minimanual of the Urban Guerrilla* (Harmondsworth: Penguin, 1971) is well known, particularly among Latin American revolutionaries.

20 Included here might be the fascist Romanian Iron Guard and Weimar Germany's Organisation Counsel. Two apparent associates of the Organisation Counsel carried out the 1921 assassination of Minister of Finance Matthias Erzberger and the 1922 assassination of Foreign Minister Walther Rathenau.

21 Crenshaw, 'Terrorism and Global Security', pp. 73–4.

22 Rami Khouri, 'Algeria's Terrifying But Unsurprising Agony', *Middle East Review*

of International Affairs, no. 5, March 1998; and Kydd and Walter, 'The Strategies of Terrorism', p. 67.

23 Combat-18's document read: 'If this is done regularly, effectively, and brutally, the aliens will respond by attacking the whites at random, forcing them off the fence and into self-defence'. Stuart Millar, 'We're At War and If That Means More Bombs, So Be It…', Guardian Unlimited, 27 April 1999, http://www.guardian. co.uk/bombs/Story/O,,204779,00.html. See also Paul Harris, 'Far Right Plot To Provoke Race Riots', *Observer*, 2 June 2001, http://www.guardian.co.uk.

24 Originally part of the Uruguayan National Liberation Movement, the group named itself Tupamaros in honour of José Condorcanqui, who led a failed revolt against Spanish rule in 1780 and was executed in 1782. The Tupac Amaru Revolutionary Movement in Peru and the Tupamaro Revolutionary Movement in Venezuela also hark back to Condorcanqui. Background on Uruguay's political development is drawn from Jeffrey Cason, 'Electoral Reform and Stability in Uruguay', *Journal of Democracy*, vol. 11, no. 2, April 2000, pp. 86–7.

25 Fernando Lopez-Alves, 'Political Crises, Strategic Choices and Terrorism: The Rise and Fall of the Uruguayan Tupamaros', *Terrorism and Political Violence*, vol. 1, no. 2, April 1989, p. 225.

26 Ironically, the Tupamaros greeted this development with pleasure, seeing military activity as evidence of the collapse of corrupt institutions and proof of their effectiveness in provoking a response. The Tupamaros switched from urban terrorism to a rural-based guerrilla strategy; this probably facilitated the military victory, as the military were trained to engage in counter-insurgency and the Tupamaros did not have extensive rural support.

27 Lopez-Alves, 'Political Crises, Strategic Choices and Terrorism', p. 225. Another source for casualty figures is the MIPT

Terrorism Knowledge Base, http://www. tkb.org. Strategies of polarisation can develop into the kind of intimidation strategies that are common in domestic terrorism when a group becomes strong enough to act as a military organisation and hold territory at least temporarily within a state. Insurgencies often use intimidation to prevent a population from supporting the government.

28 Mobilisation is not the same as an 'advertising strategy', which implies drumming up superficial, short-term attention to a cause. Mobilisation is a much more sophisticated, long-term goal of terrorist groups behaving as social movements.

29 K.G. Coffman and A.M. Odlyzko, 'The Size and Growth Rate of the Internet', *First Monday*, AT&T Labs Research, 2 October 1998, http://www.firstmonday. org/issues/issue3_10/coffman/; and World Internet Usage Statistics at http:// internetworldstats.com/stats3.htm.

30 A.T. Kearney, 'Measuring Globalization: Economic Reversals, Forward Momentum', *Foreign Policy*, no. 141, March–April 2004, pp. 54–69.

31 See, for example, Sidney Tarrow, *Power in Movement: Social Movements and Contentious Politics*, 2nd ed. (Cambridge: Cambridge University Press, 1998); and Doug McAdam, Sidney Tarrow and Charles Tilly, *The Dynamics of Contention* (Cambridge: Cambridge University Press, 2001).

32 For more on this, see Audrey Kurth Cronin, 'Cyber-mobilization: The New

Levée en Masse', *Parameters*, vol. 36, no. 2, Summer 2006, pp. 77–87.

33 This is one reason why such responses typically occur in the immediate aftermath of attacks, 'while the situation is hot', in former National Security Advisor Brent Scowcroft's words. See Michelle L. Malvesti, 'Explaining the United States' Decision to Strike Back at Terrorists', *Terrorism and Political Violence*, vol. 13, no. 2, Summer 2001, p. 95.

34 One US poll found 71% in favour of military retaliation days after 11 September. See 'Poll: Shock Gives Way to Anger', CBS News, 13 September 2001, http://www. cbsnews.com/stories/2001/09/13/archive/ main311139.shtml. On 17 September, Gallup quoted a figure closer to 90%. See 'Support for Military Action Against Terrorist Attackers', CNN.com/Community, 17 September 2001, http://archives.cnn. com/2001/COMMUNITY /09/17/newport/ index.html. A similar poll in the UK weeks later found that 70% supported military retaliation. See 'The Observer Poll Results', *Observer*, 7 October 2001, http://politics. guardian.co.uk/conservatives 2001/story/ 0,,564832,00.html. The figures in France and Italy were 68% and 88% respectively. See 'EU Leaders To Hold Emergency Summit on Security', *Daily Telegraph*, 18 September 2001, http://www.telegraph. co.uk/news/main.jhtml?xml=/news/2001/ 09/18/wdip18.xml.

35 Fear is the desired reaction on the part of the targeted population, but inspiration is the reaction intended from potential constituents.

Chapter Two

1 See Audrey Kurth Cronin, 'How Al-Qaida Ends', *International Security*, vol. 31, no. 1, Summer 2006, pp. 7–48.

2 The cases discussed here represent a sample of the full range examined in the course of the broader research project

on how terrorism ends. In that more comprehensive study, every effort has been made to include all campaigns that meet the following four characteristics: they have a political objective, use symbolic violence, purposefully target non-combatants and are carried out by non-state actors. Campaigns that primarily target military actors are not included in this study. The use of state organs to inspire terror in the state's own citizens is also excluded.

3   Figure 1 shows the distribution of lifespans across 457 groups included in the MIPT database. Selection criteria included (1) elimination of any group indicated to have targeted only property or military targets, with no indicated associated civilian or non-combatant injuries or fatalities; and (2) elimination of any group that did not display sustained organisational capabilities, that is, those groups with only one attack or with only a single series of coordinated attacks within several days of one another and with no subsequent evidence of activity or communication. These criteria removed a large number of groups that might otherwise have been included, reducing the number from 873 to 457 (in December 2006). Thus, the lifespan estimate presented here is conservative and would be even shorter if the selection criteria were more liberal. See the forthcoming *How Terrorism Ends*, Appendix.

4   For example, David Rapoport argues that 90% of terrorist organisations have a lifespan of less than one year; of those that make it to a year, more than half disappear within a decade. David C. Rapoport, 'Terrorism', in Mary Hawkesworth and Maurice Kogan (eds), *Routledge Encyclopedia of Government and Politics*, vol. 2 (London: Routledge, 1992), p. 1,067.

5   For much more on this argument, see Martha Crenshaw, 'The American Debate Over "New" Vs. "Old" Terrorism' and Audrey Kurth Cronin, 'Ending Al-Qaida: Insights from both "Old" and "New" Terrorism', papers presented at the Women in International Security (WIIS) panel, APSA annual conference, Chicago, IL, 1 September 2007.

6   Authors who hold the view that the history of terrorism does not relate to the Islamist threat include Daniel Benjamin

and Steven Simon, *The Age of Sacred Terror: Radical Islam's War Against America* (New York: Random House, 2003) and *The Next Attack: The Failure of the War on Terror and a Strategy for Getting It Right* (New York: Owl Books, 2006); Walter Laqueur, *The New Terrorism: Fanaticism and the Arms of Mass Destruction* (New York: Oxford University Press, 1999); Ian O. Lesser et al., *Countering the New Terrorism* (Santa Monica, CA: The Rand Corporation, 1999); L. Paul Bremer, 'A New Strategy for the New Face of Terrorism', *The National Interest*, November 2001, pp. 23–30; and Andrew Tan and Kumar Ramakrishna (eds), *The New Terrorism: Anatomy, Trends and Counter-Strategies* (Singapore: Times Academic Press, 2002). The concept of 'new terrorism' was introduced at the end of the millennium but gained widespread purchase after 2001.

7   The author (whose identity is unknown) urges 'jihadi fighters' to duplicate the ability of the Red Brigades and the Baader–Meinhof to compartmentalise information in order to prevent the group from unravelling. See 'Lessons Learned from the Armed Jihad Ordeal in Syria', date unknown, Harmony Document AFGP 2002-600080, reproduced in the Harmony Database, Combatting Terrorism Center, United States Military Academy, West Point, http://www.ctc. usma.edu/aq_600080.asp.

8   Harakat al-Dawla al-Islamiyya in Algeria is one of 25 'paradigmatic jihad movements' analysed by Abu Musa'b al-Suri in his 1,600-page book *Da'wat al-muqawama al-Islamiyya al-'alamiyya (The Call for Global Islamic Resistance)*, posted on the Internet in January 2005. Four of them are reviewed in detail in David Cook, *Paradigmatic Jihadi Movements*, After Action Report series edited by Jarret Brachman and Chris Heffelfinger, Combatting Terrorism Center, United States Military Academy, West Point, 2006, http://www.ctc.usma.edu.

9   Abu Bakr Naji, *The Management of Savagery*, translated by William McCants

(Cambridge, MA: John M. Olin Institute for Strategic Studies, 2006), p. 34.

10 For more on this argument, see Audrey Kurth Cronin, 'Sources of Contemporary Terrorism', in Audrey Kurth Cronin and James M. Ludes (eds), *Attacking Terrorism: Elements of a Grand Strategy* (Washington DC: Georgetown University Press, 2004), pp. 19–45.

11 To avoid endless debate and fuzzy-headed thinking about the terms 'strategic' and 'tactical' in this context, we will borrow the terms 'process' and 'outcome' from the economists. See Herbert A. Simon, 'From Substantive to Procedural Rationality', in Spiro J. Latsis (ed.), *Method and Appraisal in Economics* (Cambridge: Cambridge University Press, 1976), pp. 129–48. The meaning of 'success' (and the degree to which groups have historically enjoyed it) is explored in much greater length and depth in my forthcoming *How Terrorism Ends*.

12 Terrorist groups are typically much smaller than insurgencies, which operate as military units, hold territory (at least temporarily) and mainly target combatants. Those who rely on terrorism as a tactic normally target non-combatants and *aspire* to be guerrilla movements or insurgencies.

13 The vast majority of funding for the study of terrorism is provided by governments that are facing terrorist attacks, an important factor in the approaches taken and the research that results.

14 For example, see Gordon Corera, *Shopping for Bombs: Nuclear Proliferation, Global Insecurity, and the Rise and Fall of the A.Q. Khan Network* (Oxford: Oxford University Press, 2006); IISS, *Nuclear Black Markets: Pakistan, A.Q. Khan and the Rise of Proliferation Networks* (London: IISS, 2 May 2007); and Adrian Levy and Catherine Scott-Clark, *Deception: Pakistan, The United States, and the Secret Trade in Nuclear Weapons* (New York: Walker and Company, 2007).

15 Much more could be said about research design and case selection, but this is a policy paper. Political scientists who want a more thorough explanation of the major study from which these policy conclusions are drawn should read my *How Terrorism Ends*.

16 David Scott Palmer, 'Conclusion: The View from the Windows', in David Scott Palmer (ed.), *Shining Path of Peru*, 2nd ed. (New York: St Martin's Press, 1994), p. 261. The figures for Shining Path's decline can be verified at the MIPT database, http://www.tkb.org.

17 Notably, McKevitt's arrest was followed by the rounding up of 40 members of the Real IRA leadership.

18 The Japanese government claims that the cult currently has about 1,650 members. See Public Security Intelligence Agency, 'Review and Prospect of Internal and External Situations – Threats from Terrorism and Nuclear Proliferation and Growing Complexity in Domestic and International Situations', January 2006, pp. 51–4.

19 For published figures, see US Department of State, *Patterns of Global Terrorism 2000*, http://www.terrorisminfo.mipt.org/pdf/2000pogt.pdf; and the MIPT database, http://www.tkb.org. Subsequent to Ocalan's capture, the group renamed itself KADEK and then KONGRA-GEL (KGK), and insisted that it would only engage in political activities.

20 See James Brandon, 'Mount Qandil: A Safe Haven for Kurdish Militants – Part 1', *Terrorism Monitor*, The Jamestown Foundation, vol. 4, no. 17, 8 September 2006, http://www.jamestown.org.

21 The number of Palestinians killed through targeted killings is tallied by B'Tselem at http://www.btselem.org/english/Statistics/Casualties_Data.asp?Category=19.

22 The rate began to drop off before the 'fence' was erected, and the targeted killing policy is widely considered to be a success in Israel. Cause and effect appears to be much more complicated, however. Edward Kaplan et al. present careful data indicating that the killing of terrorist

suspects stimulated recruitment to the terror stock, arguing that preventive arrests, not targeted killings, were mainly responsible for the reduction in suicide bombings. Edward H. Kaplan, Alex Mintz, Shaul Mishal and Claudio Samban, 'What Happened to Suicide Bombings in Israel?: Insights from a Terror Stock Model', *Studies in Conflict and Terrorism*, vol. 28, no. 3, May–June 2005, pp. 225–35.

23 There is no agreement on the actual date of Khattab's death. Some report that he was allegedly killed during a clandestine Russian operation using biological toxins in March 2002. See Jim Nichol, *Russia's Chechnya Conflict: An Update*, CRS Report for Congress, no. RL31620, 16 April 2003, p. 20. On Yandarbiyev, see Peter Baker, 'Russia Moving To Eliminate Chechen Rebel Leaders; Separatists Defiant after Series of Setbacks', *Washington Post*, 20 April 2004, p. A13.

24 Ariel Cohen, 'After Maskhadov: Islamist Terrorism Threatens North Caucasus and Russia', Backgrounder, The Heritage Foundation, no. 1,838, 1 April 2005, www.heritage.org/research/russiaandeurasie/bg1838.cfm. Basayev was described in the media as 'Putin's Osama bin Laden'.

25 'Attacks Reported in Ingushetia, Stavropol and North Ossetia', *Chechnya Weekly*, vol. 8, no. 48, The Jamestown Foundation, 13 December 2007, http://jamestown.org/chechnya_weekly/article.php?articleid=2373851.

26 I am not implying that the conflict in Chechnya is strictly about terrorism. For the Chechens it involves a gradual transition from separatist insurgency to terrorism; for the Russian government, it involves a reversion to a familiar pattern of autocratic repression in responding to a threat from below. See Audrey Kurth Cronin, 'Russia and Chechnya', in Robert J. Art and Louise Richardson (eds), *Democracy and Counterterrorism: Lessons from the Past* (Washington DC: US Institute of Peace Press, 2007), pp. 383–424.

27 Kaplan et al., 'What Happened to Suicide Bombings in Israel?'.

28 A 2007 New York Police Department report indicated greater emphasis on surveillance and prevention rather than a classical criminal approach to terrorism. The arrests of 14 suspected terrorists in Barcelona in January 2008 highlight the value of prevention. Even so, such measures stop well short of ending terrorism, which is the subject of this paper. See Mitchell D. Silber and Arvin Bhatt, *Radicalization in the West: The Homegrown Threat*, New York City Police Department, 2007; and 'Spanish Terror Cell Planned Subway Attack', United Press International, 25 January 2008.

29 See Oren Gross and Fionnuala Ni Aoláin, *Law in Times of Crisis: Emergency Powers in Theory and Practice* (Cambridge: Cambridge University Press, 2006).

30 Some argue that Chechens may not have been responsible for the bombings, and charge the Federal Security Service (FSB) with carrying them out. See Michael Wines, 'A Film Clip, and Charges of a Kremlin Plot', *New York Times*, 6 March 2002, p. A8.

31 'Putin's Chechen Remark Causes Stir', BBC News, 13 November 2002.

32 The 30,000 deaths involved PKK members, civilians and members of the security forces. See Henri J. Barkey, 'Turkey and the PKK: A Pyrrhic Victory?', in Art and Richardson (eds), *Democracy and Counterterrorism*, p. 344.

33 The Truth and Reconciliation Commission, Final Report, Volume 6, *The Periods of Violence*, p. 53.

34 The Peruvian police and military, who were mostly of Spanish descent, identified their peasant targets by their darker skin. Likewise, many Russians identify Chechens by their darker complexion.

35 Al-Jihad was responsible for the 1981 assassination of Anwar Sadat. In 2001, al-Jihad merged with al-Qaeda.

36 Many point to the Palestinians' use of terrorism as an example of success; however, the argument that terrorism has advanced the cause of the Palestinian people beyond occasional tactical gains

is unconvincing. See, for example, Alan M. Dershowitz, *Why Terrorism Works: Understanding the Threat, Responding to the Challenge* (New Haven, CT: Yale University Press, 2002).

37 Kydd and Walter, 'The Strategies of Terrorism'; and Ivan Arreguin-Toft, 'How the Weak Win Wars: A Theory of Asymmetric Conflict', *International Security*, vol. 26, no. 1, Summer 2001, pp. 93–128.

38 Mia Bloom, 'Palestinian Suicide Bombing: Public Support, Market Share and Outbidding', *Political Science Quarterly*, vol. 119, no. 1, Summer 2004, pp. 61–88.

39 On this subject, see Gabriel Sheffer, 'Ethno-National Diasporas and Security', *Survival*, vol. 36, no. 1, Spring 1994, pp. 60–79.

40 Jerrold Post argues that a group must be 'successful enough in its terrorist acts and rhetoric of legitimation to attract members and perpetuate itself, but it must not be so successful that it will succeed itself out of business'. Post, 'Terrorist Psychologic: Terrorist Behavior as a Product of Psychological Forces', in Walter Reich (ed.), *Origins of Terrorism: Psychologies, Ideologies, Theologies, States of Mind*, 2nd ed. (Washington DC: The Wilson Center Press, 1998), pp. 25–40.

41 The stormtroopers in Italy and Germany engaged in organised street violence that is more reminiscent of an insurgency than classic terrorism. For an opposing viewpoint, see Mark Sedgwick, 'Inspiration and the Origins of Global Waves of Terrorism', *Studies in Conflict and Terrorism*, vol. 30, no. 2, February 2007, pp. 97–112. Sedgwick defines terrorism as 'the use of violence for the sake of its indirect political and psychological consequences by a group aiming to take political power' – a definition that omits the size and structure of the group as well as the targeting of non-combatants, and might refer as easily to insurgents and guerrillas.

42 This conclusion is drawn from careful study of 450 durable terrorist organi-sations listed by the MIPT's Terrorism Knowledge Base. Only organisations that met the requirement of sustained (repeated) attacks harming civilians through physical injury or death were included in this analysis. For thorough discussion of the data and methods, see *How Terrorism Ends*.

43 Howard Barrell has a more favourable view of MK's activities in the late 1960s, arguing that it created an 'old guard' of veterans with militant credentials who were able to assume political leadership in the 1980s – specifically Chris Hani, who both represented and pacified disgruntled MK cadres after the ANC renounced violence in 1990. Without the MK, Barrell argues that the ANC would have had even less control of events. See Howard Barrell, *The ANC's Armed Struggle* (London: Penguin Books, 1990).

44 For extensive discussion of the full range of cases, see *How Terrorism Ends*.

45 On the role of outside powers in insurgencies, see Jeffery Record, *Beating Goliath: Why Insurgencies Win* (Washington DC: Potomac Books, 2007). As examples of groups that had strong outside protectors, Walter Laqueur includes the Palestinian Arab groups and the Croatian Ustasha; see *Terrorism* (London: Weidenfeld and Nicolson, 1977), p. 118.

46 This section summarises the results of careful analysis of the negotiating behaviour of 457 groups included in the MIPT database.

47 This section deals only with negotiations over a group's fundamental goals or strategic aims that may lead to the end of a campaign. It does not analyse event-specific, tactical talks to resolve such things as hostage-takings or airline hijackings.

48 Roberts, 'The "War on Terror" in Historical Perspective', p. 109. See also John Mueller, 'Six Rather Unusual Propositions about Terrorism', and 'Response', *Terrorism and Political Violence*, vol. 17, no. 4, 2005, p. 526.

49 They may have been buying guns for a third party, as some elements of the IRA

were already mutating into organised crime groups at this point, dealing with the FARC and ETA amongst others. Conversation with Colonel Christopher Langton, IISS, March 2008.

50 Andrew Kydd and Barbara F. Walter, 'Sabotaging the Peace: The Politics of Extremist Violence', *International Organization*, vol. 56, no. 2, Spring 2002, p. 264, using data from the International Policy Institute for Counter-Terrorism database, the Interdisciplinary Center, Herzliya; and Barbara F. Walter, *Committing to Peace: The Successful Settlement of Civil Wars* (Princeton, NJ: Princeton University Press, 2002).

51 For more on this phenomenon, see David C. Rapoport, 'The Four Waves of Modern Terrorism', in Cronin and Ludes (eds), *Attacking Terrorism*, pp. 46–73.

52 Sedgwick, 'Inspiration and the Origins of Global Waves of Terrorism', pp. 97–112.

53 Cronin, 'Behind the Curve', pp. 30–58.

54 The Red Army Faction continued in a weakened form for some years and developed into what it called its 'third generation', with claims of attacks in the name of the RAF during the 1980s and early 1990s. The degree to which it truly was the same group is debatable, however.

55 Some fear that recent demographic shifts may enhance the viability of neo-Nazi groups in eastern Germany, with many more women than men going west for work, leaving a large proportion of frustrated, underemployed men reportedly ripe for recruitment. See Steffen Kroehnert, Franziska Medicus and Reiner Klingholz, 'Shortage of Women in the East', *The Demographic State of the Nation* (Berlin: Berlin-Institute for Population and Development, March 2006); and *Foreign Policy* magazine blog,

http://blog.foreignpolicy.com/node/4971?fpsrc+ealert070605.

56 On the GIA, see Michael Willis, *The Islamist Challenge in Algeria* (London: Ithaca Press, 1996); on the Provisional IRA, see Sean O'Callaghan, *The Informer: The Real Life Story of One Man's War against Terrorism* (New York: Bantam Press, 1998); and on the RAF see Donatella della Porta, *Social Movements, Political Violence and the State: A Comparative Analysis of Italy and Germany* (Cambridge: Cambridge University Press, 1995).

57 Although the April 19 Movement ended, some individuals broke away and continued to engage in violence.

58 The release of the letter spawned two new offspring, the Red Brigades/Communist Combatant Party (BR/PCC) and the Red Brigades/Union of Combatant Communists (BR/UCC).

59 Lawrence Wright, *The Looming Tower: Al-Qaeda and the Road to 9/11* (New York: Knopf, 2006), p. 258.

60 See Siobhan O'Neil, *Terrorist Precursor Crimes: Issues and Options for Congress*, CRS Report for Congress, Order Code RL34014, 24 May 2007.

61 James D. Fearon, 'Why Do Some Civil Wars Last So Much Longer Than Others?', *Journal of Peace Research*, vol. 41, no. 3, May 2004, pp. 275–301.

62 On criminality in Northern Ireland, see Marie Smyth, 'The Process of Demilitarization and the Reversibility of the Peace Process in Northern Ireland', *Terrorism and Political Violence*, vol. 16, no. 3, August 2004.

63 Here and in what follows, I have been influenced by Philip Bobbitt's excellent book *The Shield of Achilles: War, Peace and the Course of History* (London: Penguin Books, 2002).

Chapter Three

1   See Chapter 2, note 41.

2   For an interesting dissection of al-Qaeda's aims, see Max Abrahms, 'Al Qaeda's Scorecard: A Progress Report on Al Qaeda's Objectives', *Studies in Conflict and Terrorism*, vol. 29, no. 5, August 2006, pp. 509–29.

3   Among them is Michael Scheuer, a former Central Intelligence Agency (CIA) analyst and author of *Imperial Hubris: Why the West Is Losing the War on Terror* (Washington DC: Brassey's, 2004).

4   For an excellent discussion of this question, see Jason Burke, *Al-Qaeda: Casting a Shadow of Terror* (London: I.B. Taurus, 2003), pp. 13–17. Bruce Hoffman divides the organisation into four elements: al-Qaeda central; al-Qaeda affiliates and associates; al-Qaeda locals; and the al-Qaeda home-grown network. See Hoffman, 'Challenges for the US Special Operations Command Posed By the Global Terrorist Threat: Al Qaeda on the Run or on the March?', written testimony submitted to the House Armed Services Committee on Terrorism, Unconventional Threats and Capabilities of the US Congress, 14 February 2007.

5   'If a Muslim is in Britain and doesn't want to leave his job or university and go and fight Jihad on the front, what he can do is call the press agency and tell them, "I'm from the global Islamic resistance" and claim responsibility for whatever action is being done around the world.' August 2000 training video, seized in 2006, cited by Paul Cruickshank and Mohanna Hage Ali, 'Abu Musab Al Suri: Architect of the New Al Qaeda', *Studies in Conflict and Terrorism*, vol. 30, no. 1, January–February 2007, p. 8.

6   Burke, *Al-Qaeda: Casting A Shadow of Terror*, p. 39 and pp. 126–33. See also Angel Rabasa et al., *Beyond al-Qaeda*, Part 1: The Global Jihadist Movement (Santa Monica, CA: The RAND Corporation, 2006), pp. 7–22.

7   Zawahiri himself realises the danger of negotiations for the movement. 'If I fall as a martyr in the defense of Islam, my son Muhammad will avenge me, but if I am finished politically and I spend my time arguing with governments about some partial solutions, what will motivate my son to take up my weapons after I have sold these weapons in the bargains' market?' Laura Mansfield (trans.), *His Own Words: A Translation of the Writings of Dr Ayman al Zawahiri*, Part 1, 'Knights Under the Prophet's Banner' (TLG Publications, 2006), p. 128.

8   This is a discourse that is regrettably advanced by those in the West who speak of a 'clash of civilisations'.

9   Of course there is benefit in fighting the ideas at the core of the movement; however, clumsy efforts to 'empower moderates' often result in getting them killed. A more subtle approach of demystifying al-Qaeda, drawing attention to its ample mistakes, becoming much more familiar with internal schisms and pointing out inconsistencies in the debates among its associates would be more effective. Compare Rabasa et al., *Beyond al-Qaeda*, Part 1, especially the section 'Attack the Ideology', pp. 160–61. See also Fred Burton, 'The Quiet Campaign Against Al Qaeda's Local Nodes', STRATFOR, 20 June 2007, http://www.stratfor.com: '[I]t is important to remember that this is not so much a war against a group of individuals as it is a war against an ideology. The problem is, ideologies are harder to kill than people. Consider, for example, how the revolutionary ideas of Karl Marx, Vladimir Lenin and Che Guevara have outlived the men themselves.'

10 Mansfield (trans.), 'Knights Under the Prophet's Banner', p. 111. Zawahiri is referring to the Islamist movement in Egypt.

11 Radical splinter groups have been common in Islam, beginning with the Kharijites who assassinated Ali, the fourth caliph, in Iraq in the seventh

century. There is a long tradition of messianic young men giving their lives for the sake of a purer Islam. Robert F. Worth, 'Al-Qaeda's Inner Circle', *New York Review of Books*, vol. 53, no. 16, 19 October 2006, http://nybooks.com/articles/19433?email.

12 This point is very effectively developed by Philip H. Gordon, 'Winning the Right War', *Survival*, vol. 49, no, 4, Winter 2007, pp. 17–46, esp. p. 30.

13 Michael Scheuer provides a useful list of 40 groups that have announced their formation and pledged allegiance to bin Laden, al-Qaeda and al-Qaeda's strategic objectives since January 2005. See 'Al-Qaeda and Algeria's GSPC: Part of a Much Bigger Picture', *Terrorism Focus*, The Jamestown Foundation, vol. 4, no. 8, 3 April 2007.

14 For example, a 12 July 2007 communiqué issued by the new US State Department Counterterrorism Communications Center asked those who felt that any terrorist group was successfully perpetuating its message to let the Center know so that it could counter it. This point is also very well made by Burke, *Al Qaeda: Casting a Shadow of Terror*, p. 25.

15 Al-Rashid was born 'Abd al-'Aziz b. Rashid b. Hamdan al-'Anzi, but is better known as 'Abd allah b. Nasir al-Rashid. Currently in prison in Saudi Arabia, al-Rashid has been called 'a central shaper of contemporary jihadi discourse'. See William McCants and Jarret Brachman, *Militant Ideology Atlas: Research Compendium* (West Point, NY: Combating Terrorism Center, November 2006), pp. 54–6.

16 See Rita Katz and Josh Deven, 'Franchising Al Qaeda', *The Boston Globe*, 22 June 2007, http://www.boston.com.

17 Jason Burke, 'Think Again: Al Qaeda', *Foreign Policy*, no. 142, May–June 2004, pp. 18–26.

18 Ahmed Rashid, *Taliban: Militant Islam, Oil and Fundamentalism in Central Asia* (New Haven, CT: Yale Note Bene edition, 2001), p. 130.

19 It should be noted that many of the so-called 'Afghan Arabs' were neither Afghani nor Arab. One of bin Laden's contributions to the cause during the war against the Soviets was to pay rent for a building at 38 Syed Jamal al-Din Road in Peshawar, which was used as a neutral ground for talks among the bickering factions. Burke, *Al-Qaeda: Casting a Shadow of Terror*, p. 76 and fn. 32. Burke cites an interview with a former Hizb-e-Islami activist in Peshawar in October 2001. See also Rashid, *Taliban*, pp. 128–49.

20 Public-opinion polls in the Muslim world demonstrate a correlation between levels of public support for terrorism and a perceived US threat to Islam. See Ethan Bueno de Mesquita, 'Correlates of Public Support for Terrorism in the Muslim World', United States Institute of Peace Working Paper-1, 17 May 2007, www. usip.org, p. 8.

21 McCants and Brachman, *Militant Ideology Atlas: Executive Report*, p. 9.

22 This debate occurs between Salafi Sheikhs in the so-called 'Awakening Movement', including Shaikh Al-Albani, Abd al-Aziz Bin Baz, Salim al-Hilali and Rabee Madkhalee, on the one hand, and Zawahiri and other followers of Qutb ('Qutubis') on the other. See Harmony document AFGP-2002-601041, quoted and translated in Joe Felter et al., *Harmony and Disharmony: Exploiting Al-Qa'ida's Organizational Vulnerabilities*, Combating Terrorism Center (New York: US Military Academy, 14 February 2006), pp. 53–4.

23 McCants and Brachman, *Militant Ideology Atlas: Executive Report*, p. 9.

24 Jarret Brachman, 'Abu Yahya's Six Easy Steps for Defeating Al-Qaeda', *Perspectives on Terrorism*, vol. 1, no. 5, 2007, http://www.terrorismanalysts.com.

25 All of these points have been translated and analysed in the excellent McCants and Brachman, *Militant Ideology Atlas: Research Compendium*, November 2006.

26 Abu Musab Al Suri's real name is Mustafa Setmariam Nasar, sometimes shortened to Setmariam. The videotapes, dated August 2000, were recovered from

Afghanistan in 2006. See Cruickshank and Ali, 'Abu Musab Al Suri', pp. 1–14.

27 Some very fine work is being done in English in analysing these debates, notably at the Counterterrorism Center at West Point, which has for example tapped al-Qaeda's library of over 3,000 books and articles written by major movement authors, translated and analysed them, and made them available to Western researchers. This research is available at http://www.ctc.usma.edu/atlas.asp. See also Statement of Jarret Brachman before the House Armed Services Committee, Subcommittee on Terrorism, Unconventional Threats and Capabilities, Hearing on Challenges Posed to the Special Operations Command by the Global Terrorist Threat, 14 February 2007.

28 See for example *Cracks in the Foundation: Leadership Schisms in Al-Qaida, 1989–2006*, Harmony Project, Combating Terrorism Center, West Point, September 2007, http://ctc.usma.edu.

29 This is wisely recommended in Combating Terrorism Center's *Harmony and Disharmony*, p. 43.

30 This was the case with the *pentiti* of the Italian Red Brigades and the 'supergrasses' of the Provisional IRA, for example.

31 Rightly or wrongly, public perception in many parts of the Muslim world was united as a result of the Abu Ghraib and Guantanamo Bay prison debacles. Any benefit gained from interrogation of those prisoners has been dwarfed many times over by the propaganda coup handed to al-Qaeda.

32 David J. Kilcullen, 'Subversion and Countersubversion in the Campaign against Terrorism in Europe', *Studies in Conflict and Terrorism*, vol. 30, no. 8, August 2007, pp. 647–66.

33 *Ibid.*, p. 661.

34 'Knights Under the Prophet's Banner', pp. 102–105.

35 Lawrence Wright, 'The Man Behind Bin Laden', *The New Yorker*, 16 September 2002; and Wright, *The Looming Tower*, pp.

210–12. See also Jarret M. Brachman and William F. McCants, 'Stealing Al-Qaeda's Playbook', *Studies in Conflict and Terrorism*, vol. 29, no. 4, June 2006, pp. 309–21.

36 The 12 October 2002 attacks in the entertainment district of Kuta Beach killed 202 people and injured more than 200, mostly tourists. 38 of those killed were Indonesian. The attacks were orchestrated by Jemaah Islamiah, a group linked to al-Qaeda. A spokesman for al-Qaeda also claimed credit.

37 The Riyadh attacks of 12 May 2003 involved four simultaneous bombings, carried out by al-Qaeda. The majority of the casualties were Westerners, although a large number of Arab Muslims were also killed. See MIPT Terrorism Knowledge Base, at http://www.tkb.org/Incident.jsp?incID=20353.

38 Two simultaneous bombings were carried out by a Turkish al-Qaeda cell; 28 people were killed and 450 injured. See MIPT Terrorism Knowledge Base, http://www.tkb.org/Incident.jsp?incID=17488.

39 In all 191 people were killed and more than 600 injured in the attacks on Madrid's transport system. The Abu Hafs al-Masri Brigade claimed responsibility on behalf of al-Qaeda. See MIPT Terrorism Knowledge Base, http://www.tkb.org/Incident.jsp?incID=18518.

40 See MIPT Terrorism Knowledge Base, http://www.tkb.org/Incident.jsp?incID=16033 and http://www.tkb.org/Incident.jsp?incID=17375.

41 Those attacks also resulted in mass marches and shouts of 'Burn in hell Abu Musab al-Zarqawi!'. Al-Qaeda in Mesopotamia was ultimately forced to admit that the Muslim deaths were accidental, and claimed that the group would never target innocent Muslims. Its third communiqué read as follows: 'As for the Muslims who were killed in this operation, we beseech Allah to have mercy on them and forgive them, and swear that they were not the [intended] target of the operation. We did not intend, and would never have intended

for a moment, to harm them, even had they been infidels. This, assuming they were [really] in the area of the attack. The brothers who carried out the martyrdom operation meant to target the halls which served as meeting places for intelligence officers of several infidel Crusader countries and countries allied with them. The people [at the wedding feast] were killed because part of the ceiling collapsed from the intensity of the blast, and it is no secret that this was not intended; it was an unintended accident, which had not been taken into account.' See http://www.memri.org/bin/articles.cgi?Page=subjects&Area=jihad&ID=SP104305.

42 Letter from al-Zawahiri to al-Zarqawi, 11 October 2005, translated in Mansfield, *His Own Words*, pp. 268 and 271.

43 *Ibid.*, p. 273.

44 Pew Global Attitudes Project, 'Dwindling Muslim Support for Terrorism', *Global Opinion Trends 2002–2007 Report*, 24 July 2007, p. 7, http://pewglobal.org/reports/pdf/257.pdf. See also Max Abrahms, 'Why Terrorism Does Not Work', *International Security*, vol. 31, no. 2, Autumn 2006, p. 76.

45 'Dwindling Muslim Support for Terrorism'.

46 Jack Kalpakian, 'Building the Human Bomb: The Case of the 16 May 2003 Attacks in Casablanca', *Studies in Conflict and Terrorism*, vol. 28, no. 2, 2005, pp. 113–28.

47 Abrahms, 'Why Terrorism Does Not Work', p. 67.

48 Abu Yahya points out that both the Saudi and Algerian governments successfully characterised jihadist attacks in their countries as strikes not against government targets but against the people.

49 The percentage figure was derived by examining the list of casualties of each of the terrorist attacks for which al-Qaeda claimed direct responsibility between February 1993 and June 2007, and inferring the religious affiliation of the victims according to their nationalities. Only fatalities were included. The numbers were drawn from the IISS Armed Conflict Database. If Western governments are ever to develop a more effective counter-mobilisation strategy in the Muslim world, they must take the perspective of the audience into better account. Keeping track of the number of Muslim victims would be a good place to start.